2600
PHRASES
FOR SETTING
EFFECTIVE
PERFORMANCE
GOALS

Ready-to-Use Phrases That Really Get Results

PAUL FALCONE

American Management Association

New York • Atlanta • Brussels • Chicago • Mexico City • San Francisco
Shanghai • Tokyo • Toronto • Washington, D. C.

Bulk discounts available. For details visit:
www.amacombooks.org/go/specialsales
Or contact special sales:
Phone: 800-250-5308
Email: specialsls@amanet.org
View all the AMACOM titles at: www.amacombooks.org

Library of Congress Cataloging-in-Publication Data

Falcone, Paul.
  2600 phrases for setting effective performance goals : ready-to-use
phrases that really get results / Paul Falcone.
      p. cm.
  Includes bibliographical references and index.
  ISBN-13: 978-0-8144-1775-1
  ISBN-10: 0-8144-1775-2
  1. Goal setting in personnel management—Handbooks, manuals, etc.
2. Performance standards—Handbooks, manuals, etc. 3. Employee
motivation—Handbooks, manuals, etc. I. Title. II. Title: 2600 phrases
for setting effective performance goals. III. Title: Two thousand six
hundred phrases for setting effective performance goals.
  HF5549.5.G6F35 2011
  658.3'12—dc23

                                                              2011021760

About AMA

American Management Association (www.amanet.org) is a world leader
in talent development, advancing the skills of individuals to drive business success.
Our mission is to support the goals of individuals and organizations through
a complete range of products and services, including classroom and virtual seminars,
webcasts, webinars,podcasts, conferences, corporate and government solutions,
business books and research. AMA's approach to improving performance combines
experiential learning—learning through doing—with opportunities for ongoing
professional growth at every step of one's career journey.

Printing number

10 9 8 7 6 5 4 3

To my father, Carmine
For teaching me to be a man for others
and for showing me the value of
hard work, commitment, and selflessness . . .

Contents

PART II. PERFORMANCE APPRAISAL GOALS FOR PARTICULAR TITLES AND ROLES

APPENDIXES

Introduction

How to Use This Book to Save Time and to Write Compelling Performance Goals

Setting goals for your employees—or, more accurately, helping them set appropriate goals for themselves—is a very individualized and personal endeavor. Adding the right elements to the recipe, so to speak, therefore varies significantly depending on the individual's needs and aspirations. Still, your key focus always lies in customizing a blueprint or template for success to help your staff members find new ways of increasing their own productivity, which of course improves your departmental and ultimately company performance.

Creating Development Plans for Employees

So how exactly should you go about creating individual development plans for your subordinates, and, more importantly, how can this book help you get there? First and foremost, always ask your employees for their input. Without your subordinates' involvement, drafting development plans in goal statements becomes hit or miss. Second, realize that employees will remain loyal to their companies—regardless of headhunters' calls luring them away to greener pastures—as long as they're on a positive career growth trajectory and they feel appreciated for what they contribute. This so-called *psychic income* serves as the glue that binds workers to their organizations, and it's clearly the most significant element of any development plan.

If you convince subordinates that achieving specific goals at work equates to adding vivid bullets to their resumes, then you'll develop an accomplishment mentality that enables your employees not only to motivate themselves but also to reinvent themselves in light of your organization's changing needs. That's where an average manager or supervisor steps up to become an outstanding leader. Great leaders know how to set up their subordinates for success. Then they simply step aside and get out of the way.

When you describe the best bosses and mentors that you've had in your career, you're more than likely to use the verb "to be" rather than "to do." In fact, in all human relations, "beingness" typically trumps "doingness" because the greatest influencers on our lives were loving, supportive, caring, patient, and selfless in guiding us. And those traits all came much more from who they *were* than what they *did*. In other words, providing others direction and offering guidance is actually a lot easier than you think. It's simply a matter of being a selfless leader who's committed to balancing the company's needs with those of the individual worker.

If you're able to make this one paradigm shift in your belief system—that great leaders focus on *being* rather than on *doing*—you'll cut a lot of stress out of your life and develop teams that will remain very loyal to you. Loyalty begets respect, respect begets devotion, and we all know that devoted employees will give you 110% of their efforts. In short, if you command employees from the top down, you'll get no more than 100% of their efforts out of their sense of compliance. But if you can touch their hearts and help them to love you as their boss and mentor, you'll build amazingly strong teams with lots of camaraderie and teamwork and, in so doing, catapult your own career to new heights.

With these simple premises in mind, understand that you're not responsible for motivating your team. Motivation is internal, and I can't motivate you any more than you can motivate me. However, as a leader within your organization, you are indeed responsible for creating an environment in which people can motivate themselves. And that fine distinction is where this book can come in rather handy.

More Than Just a List of Descriptive Phrases

This book offers a lot more than just descriptive goal phrases outlining competencies and responsibilities. It provides wisdom and guidance on how to manage your career, lead your team more effectively, and inspire those around you to reach higher levels of individual performance and achievement. *2600 Phrases for Setting Effective Performance Goals* will provide you with insightful strategies to accomplish more yourself as well as through others, to serve as an effective career mentor and coach, and to help your company stand out from its competition. For example, when it comes to motivating and leading your team, look to phrases like these to minimize misunderstanding and open the lines of communication:

♦ Encourage individuality and foster an environment of respect and inclusion.

♦ Recognize that perception is reality until proven otherwise; therefore, always hold yourself accountable for your own "perception management."

◆ Welcome and encourage others' feedback so that they are comfortable sharing minor concerns with you before they become major impediments.

◆ Nix conversations about politics, religion, or politically incorrect, nonwork-related issues, which are sure to foster resentment or frustration.

◆ Learn what you could change about your own behavior to invoke a different response in others.

◆ Understand that building on someone's strengths makes more sense than compensating for their weaknesses.

Similarly, you can become a stronger career mentor and coach by helping your subordinates grow and develop in their own careers if you:

◆ Encourage others to engage in random acts of kindness.

◆ Find creative ways of surprising your customers.

◆ Focus on making bad relationships good and good relationships better.

◆ Look for new ways of reinventing the workflow in light of our company's changing needs.

◆ Think relationship first, transaction second.

◆ Realize that people can tell more about you by the depth of your questions than by the quality of your statements.

◆ Separate the people from the problem.

◆ Heed Mark Twain's adage: "If we were meant to talk more than we listen, we would have two mouths and one ear."

◆ Always provide two solutions for each question you ask or suggestion you raise.

◆ Employ right-brain imagination, artistry, and intuition plus left-brain logic and planning.

◆ Convert "yes . . . *but*" to "yes . . . *and*" statements to acknowledge the speaker's point of view and to share additional insights.

Likewise, recognizing that managing in corporate America today is fraught with legal peril for the unsuspecting leader, keep sage guidance like the following in mind:

◆ Never promise confidentiality before knowing the nature of the question or request.

◆ Employ the attorney-client privilege by copying our in-house counsel, asking for a legal analysis and opinion, and limiting your audience to as few individuals as possible.

◆ Recognize that the fundamental claim of *unfairness* may become the basis for a legal charge of discrimination.

Don't forget the importance of finding your own work-life balance and peace of mind as you face the daily grind and challenges that come your way throughout your career.

◆ Practice the adage, "What you want for yourself, give to another."

◆ Convince team members not to act on principle to the extent that their positions become rigid and self-justified, allowing for little compromise.

◆ Put others' needs ahead of your own, and expect them to respond in kind.

- Realize that people don't necessarily resist change; they just resist being changed.

- Accept that no one does anything wrong given their model of the world; therefore, look for common interests and underlying concerns if you need to heal a wound on your team.

- Ensure that your team communicates upward and asks for permission up front rather than for forgiveness after the fact.

- Teach what you choose to learn.

- Help your team find individual and creative solutions by asking, "I realize you don't know, but if you *did* know, what would your recommendation be?"

- Change your perspective, and you'll change your perception.

Chock full of insightful guidance and career and leadership tips, this book is packed with useful information that you can apply any time of the year, not just during performance appraisals. So sit back and let *2600 Phrases for Setting Effective Performance Goals* serve as a handy guide and guiding hand to walk you through the challenging task of helping your subordinates set not only their annual goals but also the measurable outcomes to ensure they've achieved them.

How to Use This Book

Much like the companion book, *2600 Phrases for Effective Performance Reviews*, this book attempts to serve as your ghostwriter and sage guide during the annual performance review.

Part I focuses on the characteristics and core competencies that are typically found in a company's annual performance appraisal document. Addressing matters like listening skills, communication abilities, interpersonal relations, and quantity/quality performance factors is a critical element in an individual's overall work performance. The book you now hold in your hands likewise focuses on setting specific goals around these very core competencies. The book's content works well whether you're challenged by an employee who may be a bit eccentric, quirky, or otherwise difficult to categorize and describe in writing, or whether you need specific phrases for writing your own performance goals.

Part II of this book will likewise follow the outline of *2600 Phrases for Effective Performance Reviews*, addressing goals for many of the most common positions found in corporate America today, such as sales and marketing, accounting and finance, HR, IT, legal, manufacturing, and operations. With this holistic approach toward individual performance goals as well as "role" goals for some of the most common positions in corporate America today, you'll have a cross-referencing tool to help you more clearly define your own thoughts.

The annual performance appraisal process covers both historical and forward-looking topics. The historical side looks at past performance relative to departmental and company goals as well as peer performance. The development plan, in comparison, sets the stage for future expectations and outlines the concrete and measurable outcomes that need to be reached to show that those goals were achieved.

Development plans, by definition, should be a two-way street. The exercise of obtaining agreement on the goals should be the glue between you and your employee or your boss throughout the review period. Following are some suggestions for creating individual development plans to help everyone stay engaged and self-motivated.

Tips for Setting Effective Performance Goals for Your Employees

First, get your whole team onboard with your *achievement orientation* by creating a quarterly calendar on your departmental share drive that all team members can access. This simple spreadsheet gives everyone equal ownership of documenting their key projects along with updates and completion notes so that nothing falls through the cracks, achievements are codified for everyone to see, and completion can be celebrated.

With this group production tool in hand, you need to learn what motivates each player on your team. Assuming a span of control of roughly four to eight subordinates per supervisor, this one-on-one approach should be fairly straightforward and not particularly time-consuming for you. It may, however, require a somewhat significant investment of time by your subordinates, who may want to give some very serious thought to having you help them map out their career growth plans. Here's how it might work.

At first glance, you may come across as attempting to add to your staff's already heavy workload. But this kind of work is different because it's all about them and their career interests. So don't be surprised to see your strongest players involve themselves very deeply in this exercise. After all, you're helping them fine-tune their longer-term career goals while focusing on building their skills and accomplishments now. That not only helps them when it comes time to draft their annual self-review at performance appraisal time. It also helps them add significant bullets to their resumes. And the strongest players will always be resume builders.

Determine what motivates each individual member of your team by asking them to rank-order their priorities in terms of the following six guidelines:

If you had to choose two categories from the following six, which would you say hold the most significance for you career-wise?

1. *Career progression through the ranks and opportunities for promotion and advancement*
2. *Lateral assumption of increased job responsibilities and skill building (e.g., rotational assignments in other areas, overseas opportunities, and the like)*
3. *Acquisition of new technical skills (typically requiring outside training and certification)*
4. *Development of stronger leadership, managerial, or administrative skills*
5. *Work-life balance*
6. *Money and other forms of compensation*

Consider that the sixth option, money, usually ranks fourth or fifth in exit surveys, far behind the critical areas of recognition and appreciation, open communication and respect, and opportunities for career growth and new learning. In other words, within reason, people will typically look toward the psychic income derived from working more than the money.

Also, as much as people tend to focus on money matters when making career decisions—which they very well should within reason—consider this fact: Most people who enjoy their work, who feel as though they make a positive difference, and who are otherwise at or near the top of Maslow's hierarchy in terms of self-fulfillment will stay put—despite headhunters' offers of 10–20% pay increases. Retention is what setting performance goals is all about: In the world of talent management, we keep the best and the brightest and build on their strengths.

Next, once you have individually identified the top one or two areas, shift the responsibility for reaching those goals to your employee. What can we do as a company to support you? What can I do as your supervisor to help you get there? What would it look like if this were happening for you right here and now?

Is there a risk of hearing pie-in-the-sky wish lists? Possibly. But that's easy enough to fix simply by reminding your employee about the realistic budget constraints you're under. What's more important, though, is that you're empowering your employees to develop a realistic and customized set of goals that will help them prepare for their next career move, either at your company or elsewhere.

And that last sentence isn't a mistake. Read it again: "either at your company *or elsewhere.*" Yes, selfless leadership is about helping your employees see that you're putting their needs first. And that kind of prioritization is rare to find these days in leaders. But here's the trick: People tend *not* to leave leaders whom they admire, trust, and, in many ways, love. After all, how often are they going to find managers who put their needs at the top of the list, give of themselves so willingly, and are so willing to serve as career mentors and coaches?

Do you see the paradigm shift? If you're putting their needs first, if you're coming from beingness rather than doingness, if your wisdom guides them through some of the toughest trials they might face in their jobs, they're not leaving you! And occasionally when they do for career growth reasons, you'll be happy for them because you'll know deep down that you were an instrumental part of their newfound success.

But this approach has another benefit. When you get employees thinking in terms of hard-core accomplishments and develop an achievement mentality, they learn very quickly how important it is to rack up those bullets on their resumes. Offer to review your employees' resumes with them. Teach them to use their resume as a career map and as a future guide to focus their efforts. If they're building resume bullets, they're building achievements in their annual self-reviews, which means your appraisal process becomes that much easier because they're doing all the work!

Think of this approach as the most creative aspect of leadership and management. You get an amazing amount of work done by a very focused and dedicated team. You're having fun while you're doing it. And you're teaching, by example, how your subordinates can one day in turn repay the favor by building happy, healthy, and achievement-oriented teams of their own. And don't forget all the admiration and respect that will come your way as a result of your selfless leadership style and wisdom. You'll be working less hard, getting more done through others, and garnering kudos from your own manager because of your outstanding leadership abilities.

Simply put, when you practice selfless leadership and put your team's needs first, you'll find that people will typically respond in kind. They'll work harder to demonstrate their appreciation of your leadership. They'll feel engaged and self-motivated, and they'll consequently find new ways of reinventing themselves in light of your department's changing needs. Equally as important, they'll hold themselves accountable for the end result. You can't ask for much more from any "dream team." Once you master this formula, you can replicate your success over and over again throughout your career.

And what better avenue do you have to start this engagement process than during the annual performance review? Setting future goals with your employee, as well as time frames and measurable outcomes, is what makes work fun. But setting goals once a year probably isn't enough for most people. Too many things change too quickly in business these days, and plans have to be tweaked and rearranged fairly regularly. So if setting goals based on the individual's strengths and areas of interest is the launching pad, then determining appropriate follow-up intervals is the logical next step in this yearlong trajectory.

Ask your staffers at the time of the appraisal meeting when

they'd like to meet with you again to determine progress against these goals and benchmarks. The ideal answer is quarterly: Three-month review intervals are healthy in terms of reviewing annual goals. So if a subordinate suggests a quarterly follow-up, simply ask for a calendar meeting marker for quarterly meetings spread over the upcoming twelve months.

Note that *they* send *you* the calendar invitation. *Their* career is at issue here, and you're offering to help. But always treat adults as adults, and allow them to take the lead in seeking out your guidance, not vice versa.

What if someone wants to meet in six months to review goals? That's probably okay, depending on the individual's level of independence, role knowledge, and tenure in position. My best recommendation, though, is not to allow an entire year to slip by without discussing progression toward goals, challenges, blind spots, and the like. Remember that the goal statement is in many ways the contract that binds you and your employee throughout the evaluation period. The individual development plan helps you both keep your eye on the ball, bond in overcoming unforeseen obstacles and challenges, and celebrate intermittent achievements that can be bulleted on a resume or on the employee's annual self-evaluation form.

If this sounds like the annual goal-setting process is more of a verb than a noun, you're getting the picture. Too many companies and organizational leaders see the annual performance appraisal as a *form* rather than as an ongoing *process* of engagement, interaction, achievement, and celebration. Performance appraisal becomes a mandatory annual paper chase necessary so that you can justify giving a subordinate a merit increase. And then all that paperwork goes into the individual's personnel file, never to see the light of day again until the following year. What a lost opportunity! The *process* is the point of it all!

Change your perspective, and you'll change your perception. In other words, change how you think of the annual review and goal-setting exercise, and you'll experience a totally different outcome of the power it has to focus your energies, open the lines of communication, and keep everyone on track. Seen in this light, the appraisal process is the one annual exercise that the company leadership does for its employees to help them get ahead in their careers! It's no coincidence that the process strengthens not only your company but also your own individual performance as a leader. Don't ever let an opportunity like this go to waste!

Tips for Setting Goals for Yourself

Most of us work 2,080 hours per year, and, for many of us, that's the bare minimum. But only one of those 2,080 or more hours is reserved for us. It is the one hour when we get to discuss our own assessment of how we've performed over that entire year, along with our goals for the next. And assuming your supervisor's onboard and in agreement with both your historical assessment and future game plan, then all the stars align, and we experience self-fulfillment through our work.

Now ratchet it up a notch: Instead of giving ourselves the gift of one hour per year, how about a 400% increase by giving ourselves four? In other words, what happens if we work together with a yardstick we've both agreed on to measure our personal progress and contribution to the company one quarter at a time? Personal progress and contribution to the company go hand in hand: If I'm adding skills and becoming a stronger player, then my company benefits because of my greater capabilities. I'm making a positive difference at work, and I'm keeping my skills up-to-date, my responsibilities fresh, and my resume targeted for future growth and stability.

This is a win-win-win for everybody: employee, supervisor, and company. And your yardstick—your individual development plan—should be kept front and center in your binder or notebook so that you can always remind yourself of where you're going and rethink new and faster ways of getting there. If you are a supervisor, your employees' annual goal worksheets should be front and center in *your* binder or notebook. They should act as a constant reminder of the agreements you've made and of the goals that you want to help your team members reach. They serve as a creative guidepost to help you move your employees forward faster.

Simply put, both you and your employees are focused, bonded, and working together toward a common goal. And your contract with—or your pledge to—one another sits up front in both your binders so that it can be referred to often. Congratulations! You've just learned how to maximize the power of an incredibly simple tool that enables you both to excel in your respective careers while tremendously benefiting your company.

A Final Thought

Although the examples throughout the book focus on both employee performance and conduct goals, the samples themselves can't replace the individualized goal-setting exercises outlined in this introduction. The big bang of the appraisal and goal-setting process always comes from making it an individualized and tailored action plan. That tailoring can come only from asking your employees for their input and involving them in their own career development. So, while no book can capture every individual scenario or describe every single situation, you've now got three separate ways of cross-referencing information to craft exceptional performance goals:

1. The individual's own customized development plan, which typically comes from the self-evaluation process prior to the formal appraisal (as just described)

2. A plethora of general core competencies that describe goal-setting samples for everything from leadership, teamwork, and time management to attitude, ethics, and emotional intelligence

3. A large body of role-specific goals for many of the most common positions found in corporate America, ranging from sales, finance, and IT to operations, manufacturing, and HR.

But that's not all. You'll also find the right words and descriptive phrases to communicate your thoughts and perceptions in a very concrete manner by *cross-referencing* within each group. For example, if you were looking to describe a staff member's leadership style or your own, you'd probably want to start in the chapter under leadership. But don't forget to cross-reference the chapter on supervision. For that matter, you may very well find helpful words and phrases in the sections titled personal style, staff development, conflict management and resolution, hiring and retention, and other categories listed in Part I.

Similarly, if you need to identify particular performance goals for, say, a staff accountant, that section is the logical first place to start. But also make your way over to the financial analyst, auditor, contract analyst, and controller roles. These titles vary greatly depending on the industry and on company size. So you can find additional nuggets of information in categories related to your primary target role.

At the end of the day, look to the goal-setting process as an opportunity to reinvent and strengthen your relationship with your team members and with your own supervisor. Remember, *what you want for yourself, give to another; each to his own without judgment;* and *life begins at the end of your comfort zone.* The wisdom in phrases like this can impact your entire career and outlook on life. So don't be afraid to stretch a bit here. And don't hesitate to make yourself vulnerable if you're trying something new and for the first time. You can't overcommunicate at times like these and when others sense your genuine willingness to try to make things better, you might just find that they'll respond in kind.

So enjoy the journey, and don't forget that it's all about the *process.* I hope that some of the wisdom and the strategies in this book help you master the art of performance management and leadership. More importantly, I hope they help you fall in love with helping others to build their careers and realize their ambitions. That's the greatest opportunity that the workplace offers. In fact, you can give your company no greater benefit than the gift of a motivated, energized, and engaged workforce. You're in a unique role to assist your team members in getting there, and remember . . .

Above all, teach your employees appreciation and gratitude because all good things flow from those two values.

PART I

PERFORMANCE APPRAISAL GOALS FOR CORE COMPETENCIES AND COMMONLY RATED PERFORMANCE FACTORS

Adaptability and Change Management Skills

Early Career Goals

♦ Always be ready to anticipate and adjust for roadblocks

♦ Volunteer to participate on committees and task forces to gain a more thorough perspective of the challenges facing the company

♦ Research the competition and identify two or three areas where they have distinct advantages

♦ Look for opportunities to assume greater responsibilities outside your job description

♦ Demonstrate that you can shift gears quickly and remain flexible and adaptable to change

♦ Broaden your specialty area to gain a more well-rounded understanding of the business challenges we face

♦ Forecast the five biggest challenges facing our industry and company and recommend ways to adapt

♦ Welcome change as an opportunity to learn and add new skills to your repertory

Administration/Operational Support Goals

♦ Avoid any perception of impatience or otherwise jumping to conclusions too quickly

♦ Invite constructive criticism to your responses when you disagree with a newly proposed direction or proposal

- Maintain your composure and calmness when faced with stressful changes in plan
- Welcome suggestions from those who are less familiar with a topic and benefit from their "outsider" perspective
- Become an early adapter of change by choosing a new software tool and rolling it out to the rest of the team as the subject matter expert
- View rules and regulations and policies and procedures as general structural guidelines, not as absolutes in and of themselves

Individual Contributor Goals

- Challenge new ideas constructively but see yourself as a proponent of change
- Avoid any appearance of "hanging on" while hoping to delay change enough to make it disappear
- Teach what you choose to learn
- Develop a higher tolerance level for dealing with dysfunction in the workplace
- Look for opportunities to add tools to your toolbox and expand your repertory of skills
- Appreciate the complexity of the issues we face without trying to water it down to an issue you may be more comfortable with or better understand
- Demonstrate a stronger ability to multitask and juggle competing priorities

Front-Line Supervisory and Managerial Goals

- Champion the importance of keeping yourself fresh in terms of updating your technical skills
- Be careful not to appear to jump to conclusions too quickly without having considered the merits of a proposed change in direction
- See yourself as an idea facilitator who helps others see the benefit of change
- Encourage your team to look for new and creative ways of completing even routine tasks

- Set strong but flexible achievement standards for your team
- Treat any mistakes or failures as opportunities for team growth and development

Senior Leader Goals

- Realize that people don't resist change; they just resist *being* changed
- Use gentler and softer words when critiquing someone's proposal without appearing to categorically dismiss their ideas out of hand
- Be careful to avoid being seen as overly reliant on the tried and true or otherwise caught in your comfort zone
- Avoid being labeled as defensive, stuck in the past, or resistant to change

Attendance and Punctuality (Reliability)

Early Career Goals

♦ Arrive each day fully prepared to tackle your job responsibilities

♦ Develop a reputation for reliability and excellence in all that you do

♦ Consistently follow all clock-in and clock-out procedures

♦ Arrive at the office on time and ready to begin work by your scheduled start time

♦ View reliability as a critical competency in your career development

♦ Avoid taking sick days up to the policy maximum

♦ Follow appropriate call-in procedures when reporting in sick

♦ Set the standard for attendance and punctuality on our team

♦ Strive to attain perfect attendance

♦ Always arrive at meetings on time and well prepared

♦ Comply with all company standards of performance and conduct

Administration/Operational Support Goals

♦ Strictly adhere to all break and meal periods

♦ Notify your supervisor any time you are running more than thirty minutes late

♦ Reread the company policy regarding attendance and punctuality and adhere to its guidelines

♦ Avoid patterning sick days around your weekends or holidays

♦ Arrange for temporary backup support any time you are going to be out

◆ Check in with your supervisor before you leave at night to see whether he or she needs help with anything

◆ Schedule your vacation requests well in advance of proposed leave dates

◆ Make yourself available to work last-minute overtime or weekends as necessary

Individual Contributor Goals

◆ Arrive at all meetings on time out of respect for others' time

◆ Despite your exempt status, arrive in the office by 8 A.M. and still be here at 5 P.M.—unless you've received advance approval (Being exempt does not mean you get to make your own hours.)

◆ Complete assignments and ensure that you meet deadlines on time

◆ Notify end users well in advance of a projected missed deadline

◆ Strengthen your professional reputation in regard to consistency and reliability

◆ Make up the time whenever you take an extended lunch

◆ Enroll in an effective time management course to prevent chronic scheduling challenges

Front-Line Supervisory and Managerial Goals

◆ Ensure that team members do not spend excessive time on personal phone calls or surfing the web

◆ Obtain medical documentation for any employee leaves in excess of three days

◆ Restrict medical documentation to frequency and duration only—not diagnosis

◆ Schedule time off according to tenure as outlined in the collective bargaining agreement

◆ Always maintain adequate staffing levels despite last-minute notification of employee absences

◆ Work closely with HR when dealing with employees who have intermittent FMLA (Family Medical Leave Act) claims on file

- Begin and end meetings on time
- Report any new incidents of workers' comp injuries or FMLA leave requests to HR
- Insist that nonexempt staff members leave their desks during breaks and meal periods to avoid any perception that they may be performing work (and thereby violating wage and hour rules)

Senior Leader Goals

- Process all requests for overtime, meal and rest periods, and shift differentials accurately and in accordance with company policy
- Ensure that your department adheres to all established standards for record keeping and record retention requirements
- Ensure that attendance and punctuality standards are enforced uniformly and consistently
- Notify HR any time you feel an employee may be misclassified in terms of exemption status
- Enforce all wage and hour standards to insulate the company from employment-related liability

Attitude

Early Career Goals

♦ Readily admit your mistakes or shortcomings

♦ Always remain sensitive to how you come across to others

♦ Bring out the best in people by demonstrating sincerity and care in all that you do

♦ Welcome constructive criticism as an opportunity to learn and grow

♦ Remain sensitive to how you come across to others in terms of body language and other nonverbal cues

♦ Avoid exaggeration, trash talk, obscenities, or other language that may offend others

♦ Live the mantra, "Each to his own without judgment"

♦ Be mindful of your tone of voice, body language, and posture

♦ Remain a positive influence at work, full of energy and willing to help wherever needed

Administration/Operational Support Goals

♦ Avoid drama or appearing to feed the corporate grapevine

♦ Be sensitive not to wear your emotions on your sleeve or to "let them see you sweat"

♦ Readily assume responsibility for things gone wrong without pointing fingers

♦ Remain open to new suggestions without becoming overly defensive

♦ Count to ten to regain your composure before responding to a heated question

♦ Raise your awareness level of coming across as hostile or angry toward others

♦ Welcome new ideas and approaches to how we do business

♦ Come to terms with the dysfunction that exists on our team and adjust your approach

♦ Increase your awareness of the so-called hidden org chart—the people and players who exert the most influence in the company—regardless of their current title

♦ Avoid appearing to carry a chip on your shoulder or looking angry much of the time

♦ Go out of your way to make others feel welcome, not like they're disturbing you

♦ "Great performance, bad attitude" is not an acceptable combination in this company

Individual Contributor Goals

♦ Maintain your composure even when under stress

♦ Refrain from rolling your eyeballs when you disagree with an intended course of action

♦ Never revert to sarcasm or undue criticism to express your dissatisfaction

♦ Remain a calming influence in a storm

♦ Avoid any perception of entitlement or victimization

♦ Strive to control less and delegate more

♦ Use the words "I feel" or "It made me feel" when describing hurt feelings or disappointment

♦ Remain cognizant of your reputation as a rebel producer—someone historically willing to sacrifice others to get ahead—and rebuild bridges to strengthen relationships

♦ Learn to say no and avoid spreading yourself too thin

♦ Hold yourself accountable for avoiding any perceptions of moodiness or unpredictability

♦ Recognize that certain people feel it's simply too hard to work with you and cut a wide swath around you to get things done—and make adjustments as necessary

♦ "Leave me alone—I just want to do my work" is not an acceptable approach to working successfully on this team

Front-Line Supervisory and Managerial Goals

♦ Put others' needs ahead of your own by practicing selfless leadership

♦ Be careful not to come across as insensitive or to categorically dismiss others' feelings

♦ Avoid any perception of sabotaging your subordinates by communicating your intentions up front

♦ Expect the unexpected, and plan for delays

♦ Hold your employees accountable for both their performance and conduct

♦ Act consistently, and avoid any perception of playing favorites

♦ Recognize that unfairness, especially if applied to a member of a protected group, may become the basis for a legal claim of discrimination

♦ Engaging in retaliation of any form will result in further disciplinary action up to and including immediate dismissal

♦ Refrain from making value judgments about your subordinates' intentions

♦ Address conflict head-on before minor problems become major impediments

♦ Understand that building on someone's strengths makes more sense than compensating for their weaknesses

♦ Don't allow one individual's bad attitude to contaminate the rest of your team

Senior Leader Goals

♦ Remain consistent and predictable in terms of how you handle people and problems

♦ Know that, at this organization, the end does not justify the means

♦ Avoid being seen as someone who constantly operates too close to the margins, pushes the envelope, or asks for forgiveness rather than permission

♦ Appreciate the importance of leadership and power within your organization

♦ Avoid being accused of situational ethics, that is, setting the terms of appropriate workplace conduct based on your needs at that moment

- Pick up on subtle corrective cues from others and course-correct as necessary
- Never compromise confidentiality by dropping hints to demonstrate you're "in the know" or to prove your power
- Focus on softening your bull-in-a-China-closet reputation
- Recognize the Golden Rule: All the things that proceed *from* you return *to* you (What goes around comes around.)
- Find creative ways of bringing out the best in people

Communication

Early Career Goals

♦ Readily admit that you're not sure of an answer

♦ Listen and respond to others appropriately using a respectful tone

♦ Say yes when you mean yes and no when you mean no

♦ Refrain from using comments like, "It's not in my job description"

♦ Nod your head to communicate that you are actively listening

♦ Communicate respectfully at all times, and put others' needs ahead of your own

♦ Show deference to more tenured coworkers who have contributed to the company for many years before you joined us

Administration/Operational Support Goals

♦ Manage others' expectations appropriately

♦ Answer incoming lines within two rings

♦ Do not leave callers on hold for more than 30 seconds

♦ Stop others immediately from speaking to you in a derogatory tone

♦ Comply with all budget requirements, and communicate any possible exceptions on a timely basis

♦ Never leave your manager flying blind by consistently asking yourself, "What would I need to know about this particular project if I were the manager?"

♦ Balance the quality and quantity of your workload to ensure maximum productivity

♦ Continuously look for opportunities to increase efficiency and reduce rework

Individual Contributor Goals

♦ Be conscious of your body language at all times
♦ Clearly state up front if you will not be able to deliver as requested
♦ Proactively feed information upward to keep management well informed
♦ Be careful not to appear overwhelmed or anxious about the workload
♦ Don't treat coworkers who interrupt you as if they're inconveniencing you
♦ Provide consistent feedback in a constructive manner to the engineering and design teams
♦ When dealing with others' shortcomings, always err on the side of compassion
♦ Confront people problems head-on in a constructive yet firm manner
♦ Communicate with customers using layman's English and avoiding industry jargon

Front-Line Supervisory and Managerial Goals

♦ Create a culture of openness and information sharing
♦ Build consensus via shared decision making
♦ Build trust through regular, open, and honest communication
♦ Always deliver bad news quickly and tactfully
♦ Speak persuasively and with authority, using facts and metrics to make your case
♦ Create a work environment based on inclusiveness, welcoming others' suggestions and points of view
♦ Help your staff members raise their level of awareness and sensitivity to potential employment litigation landmines
♦ Assume responsibility for problems when things go wrong, and provide recognition and praise to others when things go right

Senior Leader Goals

♦ Ensure that your direct reports are informed of each other's activities

♦ Readily share information and resources to support business objectives

♦ Avoid blaming or censuring others publicly

♦ Communicate the organization's strategic plan and its alignment with the corporate mission and values

♦ Articulate your department's strengths, weaknesses, and areas of opportunity at senior management meetings

♦ Continuously emphasize the importance of confidentiality and privacy in dealing with personnel matters

♦ Be the vision, live the values, and demonstrate excellence in all you do

Conflict Management and Resolution

Early Career Goals

♦ Heed the adage, "It's not what you say but how you say it"

♦ Put others' needs ahead of your own, and expect them to respond in kind

♦ Always develop cooperative relationships, and look for common ground

♦ Perception is reality until proven otherwise; therefore, always hold yourself accountable for your own perception management

♦ Restate the other's point of view before offering an alternative solution

♦ Make appropriate use of the human resources department and other internal resources when problems must be escalated

♦ Welcome and encourage others' feedback so that they are comfortable sharing minor concerns with you before they become major impediments

Administration/Operational Support Goals

♦ Don't automatically assume negative intentions

♦ Always look for common ground and the chance to settle disputes equitably

♦ Use silence effectively, especially when being goaded into participating in something that you don't agree with

♦ Legitimize others' points of view even if you disagree

- Depersonalize conflict whenever possible, remaining objective and above the fray
- Respect the fact that others may not have the capacity to forgive and forget as quickly as you
- Recognize that feelings aren't right or wrong—they just "are" —and use phrases like "This is how you made me feel" or "I feel very bad about . . ."

Individual Contributor Goals

- Share your concerns in a positive and constructive manner
- Avoid using demeaning terms or sarcastic or offensive humor when dealing with others
- Look for win-win opportunities to benefit both sides
- Negotiate only on merit and fairness and allow others to save face
- Know how to draw the line if you feel that your peers are not treating you properly
- Be willing to be the bearer of bad news when necessary
- Explain clearly and objectively how things appear from your vantage point so that others have a greater insight into your concerns

Front-Line Supervisory and Managerial Goals

- Don't fall prey to the adage, "The path of least resistance is avoidance"
- You have every right to observe objectively but avoid any semblance of judging others
- Ask clarifying questions and restate your position to demonstrate that you are listening
- Keep conflicts manageable by breaking issues down into their component parts and identifying areas of agreement
- Convince team members not to act on principle to the extent that rigid and self-justified positions allow for little compromise
- Avoid personalizing an issue, and always attempt to keep it objective and business-related

- Never lecture or criticize, but rather explain your point of view as objectively as possible, while respecting the other sides' opinion
- Don't allow problems to fester, and don't carry resentment with you
- Be willing to follow through with appropriate consequences, such as corrective action or termination, if a subordinate is unable or unwilling to alter behavior
- Always involve your subordinates in the solution by stating, "We have a problem that I'll need your help to fix"

Senior Leader Goals

- Address performance and conduct problems head-on
- When in doubt, always err on the side of compassion
- Avoid insensitive language like, "Why did you do that?" or "What were you thinking?"
- Recognize your ability to instill fear in others, and ensure an even playing field by welcoming others' ideas
- Accept that no one does anything wrong given his or her model of the world, and look for common interests and underlying concerns to heal a wound in your group
- Exhibit wisdom and emotional maturity when facing politically sensitive tensions
- Hold your employees to the same high expectations you hold yourself
- Be succinct in addressing problematic performance or conduct issues, and clarify your future expectations

Creativity and Innovation

Early Career Goals

♦ Rethink routine processes, and apply solutions in new ways

♦ Simplify processes, learn what works, and apply it in new ways

♦ Immerse yourself in the problem, define it clearly, and then turn it upside down before attempting to generate creative alternatives

♦ Innovation is about learning, and so learn how technologies and markets evolve and how they are linked

♦ Always look for new ways of adding customer value as an ongoing competitive advantage for the organization

♦ Innovation is the implementation of creative ideas in order to add value to the firm—learn to trust your instincts

♦ Focus on developing a reputation more as an innovation worker than as a knowledge worker

♦ Grow your career by focusing always on creativity, productivity, and efficiency

♦ Employ right-brain imagination, artistry, and intuition, plus left-brain logic and planning

♦ Avoid becoming overly consumed with marginally productive ideas

Administration/Operational Support Goals

♦ Reinvent the workflow in light of the company's changing needs

♦ Search constantly for new innovation methods, techniques, and tools

♦ Develop fresh approaches to promote your ideas and implement innovation

♦ Link innovation and creativity to business success

♦ Create and maintain a comfortable and innovative workspace that allows for more effective brainstorming and streams of consciousness

♦ Enhance your workplace relationships with peers to encourage greater collaboration, creativity, and open discussion

♦ Generate fresh solutions to problems that will allow us to create new products, processes, or services for a changing market

♦ When generating creative ideas, give freedom early, create structure later

Individual Contributor Goals

♦ Constantly focus on linking technology decisions with business strategy

♦ Trust your intuition and rely on your knowledge

♦ Think outside the proverbial box, and, in some cases, feel free to blow the box up

♦ Generate ideas without judging them

♦ Outperform the competition by generating breakthrough ideas

♦ Consider innovation in the workplace part of your ongoing responsibilities in order to train yourself to deal with change in a new way

♦ Evaluate ideas for viability, develop them into concepts, and turn them into reality

♦ Think new product ideas all the way through, from developing prototypes to testing functionality to setting up production facilities to seeking suppliers

♦ Gain new perspectives from your peers and likewise provide constructive input into others' ideas and suggestions

♦ Turn ideas into action, put creativity to work, and develop strategies for innovation

♦ Reinvent the process flow in order to integrate supply-chain design with concurrent engineering

♦ Look constantly for parallels, patterns, variations, and analogies

♦ Experiment by adding, combining, and clarifying

Front-Line Supervisory and Managerial Goals

♦ Make it safe for your team to take risks

- Engage talent within the organization and across the value chain
- Establish diverse project teams to bring a broader range of knowledge, experience, thinking, and creativity to the table
- Ensure that your team communicates upward and asks for advanced permission rather than forgiveness afterward
- Always look for new ways of increasing revenue, decreasing costs, and saving time
- Recognize and reward your employees' desire to suggest alternatives, to assume responsibility, to achieve, and to succeed
- Refer more to wikis, blogs, and shared documents that encourage collaboration and group input
- Enhance team creativity by conducting high-performance brainstorming sessions
- Learn what current relationships, moods, and conversations are thwarting your group

Senior Leader Goals

- View all employees as leaders, innovators, and change agents
- Deliberately and consciously create a culture of change
- Offer advanced training, educational, and career development opportunities to spur creative suggestions and solutions
- Drive breakthrough innovations in technology and operations management, and deliver them on a world-class level
- Ensure cross-enterprise collaboration by creating ad hoc virtual teams that involve different functions, levels, and disciplines
- Drive strategic innovation to leverage learning and collaboration opportunities with customers, lead users, and suppliers
- Develop alternative strategies for coping with shorter product life cycles, while delivering greater customer satisfaction
- Maximize worker involvement in planning, decision making, and operating procedure to spur creativity
- Gain competitive advantage through creative problem solving
- Recognize that creativity is the number one leadership competency of the future

Customer Satisfaction

Early Career Goals

♦ Anticipate customer needs by placing yourself in your customers' shoes

♦ Provide knock-your-socks-off service

♦ Look constantly for new ways of adding value to the customer relationship

♦ Think relationship first, transaction second

♦ Prepare unique responses to the three most common objections you receive

♦ Articulate what makes this company stand out from the competition

♦ Repeat business equals long-term cash flow and is the key to success

♦ Exceed customer expectations by providing timely feedback and follow-up

♦ Always put the client's needs above your own

Administration/Operational Support Goals

♦ Expect customers to complain more than compliment

♦ Provide timely metrics and analytics reports to drive sales strategy

♦ Identify the source of the three most common complaints and prepare front-end solutions to address them proactively

♦ Provide thorough product support documentation and training to ensure that team members fully understand what they're selling

♦ Never appear to talk down to or patronize customers

♦ Refrain from speaking poorly of the competition

♦ Tactfully tell customers *no* when their demands or expectations are unreasonable or can't be met

Individual Contributor Goals

♦ Study the competition so you know what you're up against

♦ Find creative ways of remaining in touch with your clients by providing value-added information that helps them do their jobs better

♦ Bring your clients together over lunch to help them develop a network in their field

♦ Be willing to help in areas where you won't necessarily earn a commission

♦ Find creative ways of surprising your customers

♦ Become a reliable resource that customers can count on for objective and selfless advice

♦ Forecast what your customers will want and expect

♦ Consistently meet all performance benchmarks contained in your cycle scorecard

♦ Distinguish between features and benefits in order to successfully overcome objections

♦ Sell the product on a problem-to-solution level

♦ Never use pressure to close a deal or to unduly influence a customer's decision

♦ Follow up with customers after the conclusion of a sale to ensure their satisfaction

Front-Line Supervisory and Managerial Goals

♦ Conduct postmortems on any lost customers to see how you could have retained them

♦ Make your leading client developers subject matter experts who share best practices with their peers

♦ Balance quality ratios with raw outbound call numbers to ensure that team members are working smarter, not harder

♦ Role-play opening statements, initial objections, and closing strategies with new hires

- Ensure that new hires plan their work and work their plan, using daily call sheets
- Never permit customers to abuse your employees or treat them poorly

Senior Leader Goals

- Link organizational profit and growth directly to customer satisfaction and repeat business
- Look for continuous improvement opportunities in the customer relationship
- Track and trend patterns of new and lost customers among competitors
- Institutionalize successful customer transactions by documenting key deal points and closes
- Redesign the process workflow to better meet clients' needs
- Look for new ways of differentiating this organization from the competition

Diversity Orientation

Early Career Goals

- Seek out the opinions of others who at first glance may not have much in common with you
- Respect others' points of view and honor their opinions
- Nurture your network by finding common ground with peers and associates
- Demonstrate empathy and caring when dealing with your peers
- Put others' needs ahead of your own, and expect them to respond in kind
- Raise your awareness in terms of reading other people's feelings and moods
- Don't rush to judgment—wait until you've truly listened and fully heard another's point of view

Administration/Operational Support Goals

- Be sensitive to how you're coming across, and avoid any perceptions of arrogance or condescension
- Recognize each individual's unique contribution to your team
- Appreciate that everyone brings unique attributes and experiences to the table
- Nix conversations about politics, religion, or other politically incorrect nonwork-related issues that are sure to foster resentments or frustration
- Avoid any appearance of direct attack or premature assessment
- Make a conscious decision to make everyone feel like a valued member of the company

Individual Contributor Goals

♦ Always create a positive and inclusive work environment

♦ Respectfully challenge others' recommendations by providing a full explanation of your logic and reasoning

♦ Put people first to encourage creative problem solving and to build camaraderie

♦ Listen with full eye contact and body language

♦ Look always for similarities rather than differences when building relationships at work

♦ Involve and value everyone regardless of his or her differences

Front-Line Supervisory and Managerial Goals

♦ Create an inclusive work environment where all team members feel welcome to share their ideas and suggestions

♦ Celebrate your differences and view them as a strategic advantage

♦ Rely on your differing points of view and life experiences to create enriched solutions that appeal to a broader mass of customers

♦ Welcome dissenting opinions, and encourage respectful challenges to the status quo

♦ Don't confuse having high expectations with a license to railroad others or remain insensitive to their feelings or needs

♦ Encourage constructive debate and dialog to teach your team how to think through a problem and proffer a reasonable solution

♦ Avoid conduct that may constitute harassment of any protected class

♦ Demonstrate caring leadership by remaining sensitive to others' needs

♦ Focus always on bringing out the best in others

Senior Leader Goals

♦ Recognize diversity as a critical business issue

♦ Make attracting, developing, and retaining a diverse workforce a key strategic imperative for your division

♦ Encourage individuality, and foster an environment of respect and inclusion

♦ Identify the barriers to inclusion that may plague your workforce

♦ Ensure that the work environment aligns with the organization's mission and values surrounding diversity and inclusion

♦ Offer diversity awareness training and diversity skills training to all front-line supervisors as a core workshop

♦ Constantly assess your culture and organizational climate to ensure that it is welcoming to all

♦ View diversity as a strategic business imperative

♦ Look for opportunities to tie diversity and inclusion to your business strategy in order to increase performance, productivity, and customer retention

Emotional Intelligence

Early Career Goals

♦ Seek to acquire new perspectives in order to broaden your view

♦ Separate the person from the problem, and withhold judgment

♦ Empathize with others, knowing that no one does anything wrong given his or her model of the world

♦ Learn from your mistakes and simply view them as the cost of tuition in this school called the business world

♦ Don't be so hard on yourself, and learn to forgive others by not bearing a grudge

♦ Celebrate successes, and share the credit with others

♦ Challenge yourself to learn and grow by focusing on building achievements into your resume

Administration/Operational Support Goals

♦ Always look to be a calming influence when dealing with conflicting groups

♦ Remain adaptable and flexible to meet the needs of the moment

♦ Empower others by allowing them to share ownership and visibility

♦ Raise your awareness level of what motivates others—money, recognition, promotional opportunities, integrity, and the like

♦ Focus on making bad relationships good and good relationships better

♦ Readily assume responsibility for your mistakes, and immediately inform anyone who may be impacted

Individual Contributor Goals

♦ Learn what you can change about your own behavior to invoke a different response from others

♦ Practice the simple courtesies of listening attentively, remaining approachable, and welcoming others' suggestions

♦ Frame your questions properly, and brainstorm alternatives to resolve problems

♦ Teach what you choose to learn

♦ Regularly seek corrective feedback, and make it safe for others to speak openly with you

♦ Remain sensitive to nonverbal cues and the unspoken dialogue of body language

Front-Line Supervisory and Managerial Goals

♦ Create disparate groups of problem solvers to generate fresh ideas and solutions

♦ See yourself always as a coach and mentor rather than as a unilateral decision maker and disciplinarian

♦ Make it safe to take risks and welcome bad news

♦ Avoid gripe sessions by insisting that staff members provide two solutions for each question they raise or request they make

♦ Help your team find individual and creative solutions by asking, "I realize you don't know, but *if you did know*, what would your recommendation be?"

♦ Focus your team on generating concrete achievements and accomplishments by asking them to prepare quarterly performance appraisal updates for your review

♦ Create an environment where people can motivate themselves

♦ Set people up for success by clearly communicating the desired end result and then providing full autonomy to complete the task

♦ Catch people being good, and celebrate successes

♦ Surprise subordinates with challenging assignments

♦ Allow staffers to participate in setting individual goals and give them the freedom to control reaching those goals

Senior Leader Goals

♦ Understand that wisdom is knowledge applied, and so look always to provide wisdom and sage guidance to your organization

♦ Change your perspective, and you'll change your perception

♦ Avoid speculating or getting too far off target

♦ See yourself as a strategist and visionary

♦ Communicate often, and demonstrate appreciation and recognition of others' contributions

♦ Show a personal interest in people's personal lives and career goals

♦ Deliver tough messages in a compassionate manner

♦ Above all, teach your employees appreciation and gratitude because all good things flow from those two values

Ethics, Integrity, and Trust

Early Career Goals

♦ Treat others with dignity and respect at all times

♦ Confidentiality is critical; share information carefully and on a need-to-know basis

♦ Your reputation is the coin of the realm in corporate America

♦ Demonstrate integrity and character in the face of overwhelming challenges

♦ Never underpromise and overstay your welcome in someone else's office

♦ Always disclose the full picture of your intentions so that others understand your motives and end goals

♦ Walk the talk of your convictions, and strive to remain consistent

Administration/Operational Support Goals

♦ Proactively feed information up the chain of command so that no one could accuse you of withholding or limiting it

♦ Return all phone calls in a timely manner regardless of the caller's rank or status in the company

♦ Minimize any perception of failing to want to make a decision or push responsibility to someone else

♦ Avoid stretching the truth or embellishing your statements

♦ Remain sensitive to how you may come across to others from different backgrounds or cultures

♦ Heighten your awareness of your communication style

♦ Make no promises that you're not fully in control of keeping

Individual Contributor Goals

♦ Disclose any potential conflicts of interest in a timely manner

♦ Publicly acknowledge your mistakes, and assume personal responsibility

♦ Don't avoid conflict in hopes that a problem will resolve itself

♦ Make known any project concerns you have that could blindside or embarrass others

♦ Set others up for success by creating an environment where people can motivate themselves to assume broader responsibilities

♦ Place others' needs ahead of your own, and expect them to respond in kind

♦ Be careful about overstepping your boundaries by skipping tiers of management in an effort to get to the people at the top

Front-Line Supervisory and Managerial Goals

♦ Never promise confidentiality before knowing the nature of the question or request

♦ Qualify any subordinates' requests for up-front confidentiality with the following caveat: "If it has to do with (1) discrimination or harassment, (2) potential violence in the workplace, or (3) a potential conflict of interest with the company, I have an obligation to disclose it to upper management"

♦ See yourself as a role model for those around you

♦ Set the tone for acceptable conduct, and look beyond the letter of the law to the spirit of a specific policy or workplace rule

♦ Become more transparent with your staff members in terms of explaining why they need to do things and how they can help move the ball forward

Senior Leader Goals

♦ Resist any urge to come from the information-is-power school of thought

- Engage your employees in open book management, where you provide them with the bigger picture and enlist their help and support in determining solutions

- Manage with a conscience by building trust, integrity, and commitment in the workplace

- Create an ethical workplace by practicing selfless leadership

- Avoid perceptions of favoritism or inconsistent treatment

- Hold employees accountable to a high standard of performance, and avoid any semblance of drama when addressing individual shortcomings

- Make an effort to get to know your subordinates' needs and help them excel in their careers and within the company

Hiring and Retention

Early Career Goals

♦ *Not applicable*

Administration/Operational Support Goals

♦ Strengthen your interviewing skills to assess candidates more effectively

♦ Make candidates feel comfortable enough to reveal their true selves and not keep discussions at arm's length

♦ Ask applicants to self-assess how their skills match your open position

♦ Broaden the pool of candidates by employing a full spectrum of outreach sources, including ads, referrals, and direct sourcing

♦ Dedicate an appropriate amount of time to each interview meeting

♦ Make use of social media, including LinkedIn, Facebook, and Twitter, to source passive candidates who may not be looking for a job change

♦ Ensure that you have enough questions in your arsenal to add critical mass to your interview

♦ Never leave candidates waiting in the lobby for more than 20 minutes without addressing the reason for the delay

♦ Compete for talent by focusing on retaining the best and the brightest

♦ Retrain and retool any team members who have let their skills lapse because of lack of use

♦ Don't rush to replace people who may be able to turn themselves around with a reasonable amount of skill building

♦ Coach, mentor, and guide talented team members who are hungry to learn

♦ Build a new hire orientation program to successfully transition recruits into the company

♦ Training and skill-building opportunities create the learning curve, and being in the learning curve leads to greater employee engagement and retention

Individual Contributor Goals

♦ *Not applicable*

Front-Line Supervisory and Managerial Goals

♦ Surround yourself with people who possess a proven accomplishment mindset

♦ Develop a success profile with specific competencies to evaluate consistently

♦ Value talent as a scare resource and a differentiator of ultimate success

♦ Ask behavioral interview questions to get candidates off their scripted responses

♦ Employ a full arsenal of interview questioning categories, including traditional, holistic, and pressure cooker queries

♦ Look for ways to lower your department's turnover to the company average of 16%

♦ Avoid potentially discriminatory questions at all costs

♦ Partner with your recruiter in HR to speak with candidates' prior supervisors during the reference checking process so that you can hear firsthand about strengths, weaknesses, and areas for development

♦ Be aware that all employment offers must be extended through human resources

- Ensure that your interview note taking is in no way linked to any type of protected category, including age, race, gender, sexual orientation, and the like
- If possible, promote internally first, and then post the backfill position
- Measure new hire turnover, specifically through the 90-day probation period
- Analyze the reasons for leaving for both voluntary and involuntary terminations
- Recognize that workers "join companies and leave supervisors"— and see yourself as the glue that binds someone to the organization

Senior Leader Goals

- Recognize that attracting and developing top talent remains your key responsibility
- Ensure that diversity outreach is a critical part of each search campaign
- Institute exit interviews to analyze primary versus secondary reasons for leaving
- Master the art of matching a candidate's personality to your corporate culture
- Look to fill positions internally first before going outside the company
- Post all positions according to the collective bargaining agreement even if you've identified someone internally for promotion
- Minimize your reliance on executive search firms, and keep a close eye on cost-per-hire metrics
- Hire people who are smarter than you, and get out of their way
- Build career progression plans for all technicians that raise the base salary rate as new skills are formally acquired
- Implement an employee opinion survey to gauge employee satisfaction
- Don't feel as though you have to interview a thousand candidates before making a selection decision
- Be patient, and don't rush to hire the first candidate who walks in the door

- Appreciate diverse talents and backgrounds, and avoid hiring only "in your own image"
- Value succession planning as a key executive leadership responsibility
- Recognize that people leave companies for one of three reasons—the lack of (1) recognition and appreciation, (2) communication from their immediate supervisor, and (3) internal growth opportunities—and build a retention program to satisfy those three critical needs

Job Knowledge

Early Career Goals

- Realize that people respect competence
- Focus on demonstrating mastery in your key areas of responsibility
- Outline your conceptual understanding of your business and industry
- Craft checklists to structure your thoughts when looking at a business problem
- Always think issues through to their logical conclusion
- Make sure you understand the ins and outs of the business you're in
- Identify your company's two biggest income streams and three largest expense drivers
- Nurture your network of industry contacts and career mentors
- Keep abreast of trends and changes in the industry
- Read the annual report to better understand the financial drivers and strategic initiatives that influence day-to-day operations
- Don't settle for marginal work, and ensure that your work stands out
- Challenge yourself to go above and beyond basic expectations
- Consistently demonstrate mastery of basic concepts in your area of responsibility

Administration/Operational Support Goals

- Consistently hit all performance targets and role objectives from this point forward

- Avoid asking basic, repetitive questions that you should already know the answers to
- Review and update your current job description to be sure you understand the primary versus secondary responsibilities expected of you
- Plan your work and work your plan accordingly
- Focus on doing things right and doing the right things
- Avoid producing a substandard or untimely work product
- Broaden your perspective beyond just your profession and function to include your organization as well as your industry
- Look to serve as the resident expert for administration and training initiatives
- Avoid making excessive errors in light of your many years of experience in your field
- Join the appropriate national association, and purchase its magazine to bring yourself up to speed about doing business in your industry
- Identify the core competencies that your organization needs to succeed
- Volunteer for task force opportunities that will broaden your exposure to other functions, disciplines, and roles within your company
- Invest the energy necessary to get stellar results
- Sign up for internal training courses and independent study

Individual Contributor Goals

- Identify the skill gap that's holding you back from excelling in your role
- Show a greater interest in exploring self-development opportunities
- Remain open to constructive feedback
- Take advantage of side-chair meetings where you can observe peers in different areas of your company and learn about the challenges they face
- Develop goals based on your understanding of business priorities
- Analyze the company's balance sheet and income statement for specific vulnerabilities or areas the firm should focus on
- Increase your knowledge of key players at competitor firms

- Get closer to customers to see the business through their eyes
- Study the competition to learn how your company should differentiate itself
- Always take a strategic-business-partner approach to your work
- Don't resist suggestions for doing things in a different way or using an alternative approach
- Broaden and diversify your specialist credentials into more of a generalist role
- Be careful not to overly rely on a single skill that got you to this point in your career
- Differentiate key priorities from activities that are less critical
- Design your work processes to maximize efficiency and effectiveness
- Actively transfer your knowledge to junior staffers

Front-Line Supervisory and Managerial Goals

- *Not applicable*

Senior Leader Goals

- Know your budget limits before committing to a new project or initiative
- Gain a greater understanding of the mission-critical focus areas outside your immediate department
- Forecast your business needs based on emerging trends and new technologies
- Develop a stronger opinion regarding our organization's strategic planning initiatives
- Link the mission-critical goals of your area with the capabilities of the talent already in place to determine whether you have the right people in the right roles
- Don't get mired in tactics and details, losing sight of the bigger picture
- Demonstrate a natural curiosity about where the business is heading and how you can help get it there
- Teach what you choose to learn so that you can learn it yourself

- Attend other departments' offsite meetings to learn of their goals and challenges
- Conduct a SWOT analysis of your company's strengths, weaknesses, opportunities, and threats
- Raise the bar, and set your team's goals higher
- Deal with stress and pressure appropriately without appearing to become overwhelmed
- Gain better and more reliable access to the resources your team needs to succeed
- Be careful not to develop a reputation as a crisis manager, that is, someone who performs well only on the fly when no preparation or strategic thinking is involved

Leadership

Early Career Goals

♦ Lead always by example

♦ Be the first to volunteer to help others succeed

♦ See yourself as a model of sharing, cooperation, and goodwill

♦ Share successes, and assume responsibility for errors and short-comings

♦ Increase your own sense of self-satisfaction by sharing your talents freely

♦ Practice the adage, "What you want for yourself, give to another"

♦ Engender trust and respect among your teammates

♦ Volunteer for leadership opportunities in industry and charity events

Administration/Operational Support Goals

♦ Concede minor points in an effort to allow others to save face

♦ Be a source of stability and calmness when angst and pressure abound

♦ Look for ways to stand out as a rarity among your peers

♦ Avoid being the source of surprises

♦ Build relationships within and across departments

♦ Be cognizant of the nonverbal cues you may sometimes give off

♦ Increase your sense of self-awareness, and hold yourself accountable for your own perception management

♦ Realize that people can tell more about you by the depth of the questions you ask than by the statements you make

Individual Contributor Goals

♦ Shed light on common goals, challenges, and organizational impediments

♦ Stop negative personal styles from blocking group performance

♦ Practice MBWA (management by walking around)

♦ Welcome criticism of your ideas

♦ Always provide two solutions for each question you raise

♦ Listen openly and look for common ground

♦ Make others feel welcome to seek your advice and counsel

♦ Feel safe to make mistakes and volunteer new ideas

♦ Avoid sharp reactions or instant retorts that may put others off

Front-Line Supervisory and Managerial Goals

♦ Establish and communicate effective goals and measures

♦ Celebrate successes, and learn from mistakes

♦ Conduct post mortems to make opportunities out of failures

♦ Use stretch goals to increase both performance and motivation

♦ Always err on the side of compassion

♦ Accept the dictum, "Each to his own without judgment"

♦ Separate the person from the problem

♦ Create high-performance teams by creating a work environment in which employees can motivate themselves

♦ Enroll in a course on creating a high-performance organization

♦ Build trust through regular, open, and honest communication

♦ Create a continuous learning environment

Senior Leader Goals

♦ Practice selfless leadership by placing others' needs ahead of your own and expecting others to respond in kind

♦ Focus on aligning each member of your team by setting a common vision

♦ Strive to provide a healthy work-life balance for members of your department

♦ Engage your team in setting specific, measurable goals and concrete outcomes

♦ Observe objectively without rendering judgment

♦ Identify the most common problems that hinder peak performance

♦ Provide open-book leadership so that your team understands the financial and operational drivers of organizational success

♦ Coach people to prepare for their next move in career progression

Listening Skills

Early Career Goals

- Listen objectively and with an open mind
- Give whoever is talking your undivided attention
- Strive to maintain full eye contact and eliminate mental and physical distractions
- Anticipate what the speaker is going to say in an effort to stay on top of the discussion
- Realize that you can't hear if you do all the talking

Administration/Operational Support Goals

- Count to two before responding so as not to interrupt another's final thoughts or concluding statements
- Take accurate notes, and ask clarifying questions any time you are unsure of my directions
- Read between the lines, and always look for nonverbal cues
- Summarize key points and details to yourself if your mind begins to stray
- Heed Mark Twain's adage, "If we were meant to talk more than we listen, we would have two mouths and one ear"

Individual Contributor Goals

- Realize that you cannot listen effectively if you are anticipating what you will say and waiting for a break to jump in
- Paraphrase to clarify what the speaker has said

♦ Ask open-ended questions to ensure that the speaker is aware that you are engaged in the conversation

♦ Refrain from demonstrating overtly negative feelings when dissatisfied with a staff member's response or recommendation

♦ Listen with empathy, and try to see the situation from the other person's point of view

Front-Line Supervisory and Managerial Goals

♦ Bear in mind that hearing is a passive action and that listening is active

♦ Face those you are talking with and make eye contact to demonstrate your interest and concern

♦ Nod your head, and use the appropriate body language when listening to make the other person feel important and recognized

♦ Convert "yes . . . *but*" to "yes . . . *and*" to acknowledge the speaker's point of view and to share additional insights

♦ Nod in agreement, smile at jokes, and indicate confusion so the listener knows to restate a point

Senior Leader Goals

♦ Be alert to what is left unsaid

♦ Avoid stereotyping so that you will not bias your listening

♦ Strive not only to listen to others' words but also to assess their tone of voice and body signals in order to understand their full message

♦ If you hear something that you don't agree with, try not to react immediately or disengage, but get as much information as possible before drawing a conclusion

♦ Be cognizant not to talk over subordinates or interrupt them

♦ Consider that most people can speak approximately 100 words per minute, but they can think 400 words per minute; so don't overly anticipate or allow prejudgment to bias the message

Managerial Style

Early Career Goals

♦ *Not applicable*

Administration/Operational Support Goals

♦ *Not applicable*

Individual Contributor Goals

♦ *Not applicable*

Front-Line Supervisory and Managerial Goals

♦ Bring out the best in people by demonstrating care and concern about their well-being

♦ Remain passionate about the work you do and about the people you interact with

♦ Structure your day and organize your office to avoid getting overwhelmed

♦ Recognize your perfectionism and learn that fault-free, no-risk decisions are a luxury we can't afford to take

♦ Discipline yourself to get work done more efficiently and effectively

♦ Share freely when you're feeling anxious, frustrated, or upset so that others don't have to divine by your actions that you're not coming from a good place

- Wrap up completed projects in nice, clean packages
- Remain consistent in your application of company policy and practices
- Recognize that sometimes the best you can do is to move things forward incrementally without necessarily completing what you're working on
- Depersonalize conflict by separating the person from the problem
- Show patience, and develop common ground with people you don't agree with
- Manage up more effectively by keeping your supervisor apprised of important issues that he or she will probably be asked about
- Find new and creative ways of motivating yourself and others to excel and reengage
- Avoid coming across as tense, impatient, or impersonal when working with direct reports
- Conduct corporate battles appropriately by evening the playing field and inviting a third party like human resources to objectively broker the meeting
- Keep all the necessary parties involved and gain advanced buy-in when rendering a decision that may have precedent-setting value
- Volunteer for community service activities, and find ways of giving back
- Become a source of advice and counsel during times of crisis
- Demonstrate business maturity and emotional intelligence when things hit the fan
- Catch people being good, and practice random acts of kindness
- Resolve conflict properly by asking clarifying questions and restating the other's position
- Implement higher standards for your team, and don't allow excessive excuses
- Know when to draw the line so that problems and ill will don't fester
- Communicate in advance any potential deviations from standard operating procedures
- Don't shy away from dealing with employees who have poor attitudes
- Be cautious not to overinflate grades during the annual performance review process

- View delegation as the key to developing your staffers and preparing them for their next logical move in career progression
- Be careful not to exaggerate, generalize, or interpret opinions and assumptions as facts
- Don't jump to decisions just to do something or to act without thinking through the consequences
- Don't appear to isolate yourself by closing your door or communicating only via e-mail and instant messaging
- Discourage subordinates from unfounded speculation about private matters

Senior Leader Goals

- Model the highest ethics, values, and integrity
- Create a culture of genuine caring, compassion, and empathy
- Create a culture of open information sharing and increased accountability
- Become more proactive at dealing with ambiguity and uncertainty
- Think twice before rejecting precedent and history
- Design intermittent feedback loops to gauge the progress of a project, and be prepared to course-correct as necessary
- Understand what triggers your emotional hot buttons
- Look for training workshops that will help you navigate the rapids of corporate politics more successfully
- Work on building rapport by putting in an extra effort to make others feel welcome
- Be careful not to be overly optimistic about your staff's abilities
- Recognize your reputation for keeping others at arm's length and at a distance
- Know that your ability to instill fear in others is both a blessing and a curse
- Be aware that you could be held legally liable for managerial "bad acts" and for acting outside the course and scope of your job description
- Avoid any appearances of arrogance, insensitivity, or judgment of others

- Be careful not to engage in sharp reactions that make people gun-shy to take risks
- Don't be afraid to take a tough stand or to face conflict and crisis head-on
- Communicate a compelling and inspired vision
- Allow others to save face by conceding small points and meeting them halfway
- When dealing with a crisis, realize that you can't overcommunicate
- Focus on building the *gravitas*, confidence, and leadership presence necessary to hold an audience's attention
- Don't delegate work that you should rightly do yourself
- Recognize diversity as a key business strategy, and create an inclusive work environment
- Don't be too quick to replace subordinates; look for opportunities to grow and develop them instead

Motivation

Early Career Goals

- Always treat others with respect and dignity, and expect them to respond in kind
- Realize that if you love what you do, you'll never have to work a day in your life
- Place yourself into situations where you can learn and simultaneously give back
- Demonstrate passion not only for your work but also for the co-workers whose lives you touch
- Act with sincerity by placing others' needs ahead of your own
- Assume good intentions unless and until proven otherwise

Administration/Operational Support Goals

- Make promotions-from-within a primary staffing and development goal
- Keep the lines of communication open so that team members share concerns openly
- Get to know staffers personally by learning two to three personal things about each one
- Help your subordinates develop their resumes by adding both new technical skills and concrete achievements—a win-win for both employee and company
- Understand that recognition and communication are the two key reasons why top performers remain with any company
- Set clear goals with predefined follow-up points, and then get out of their way

♦ Follow the simple rule, "What you want for yourself, give to another"

♦ Avoid any perceptions of favoritism or inconsistent treatment

Individual Contributor Goals

♦ Listen with a genuine intent to understand others' points of view

♦ Help others reach their personal best in a spirit of positive cooperation

♦ Encourage teamwork and group learning by sharing your knowledge freely

♦ Provide feedback in a constructive and caring manner

♦ Always follow up and deliver on the commitments that you make

♦ Teach what you choose to learn

♦ Share any concerns objectively and without drama

♦ Communicate candidly and openly about needed course corrections

♦ Perform postmortems on deals gone badly, and view mistakes as key learning opportunities

Front-Line Supervisory and Managerial Goals

♦ Personally and publicly congratulate subordinates for demonstrated achievements

♦ Structure your expectations clearly by mapping out the finished product on paper

♦ Encourage employee input and creativity

♦ Keep your door open at all times when you're alone in your office

♦ Ask your employees what motivates them, and then ask them how to help you get them there

♦ Build morale by celebrating group successes

♦ Provide consistent and timely feedback as a key development tool

♦ Focus always on employee engagement by fostering a workplace based on trust, recognition, and mutual respect

♦ Celebrate both group and individual successes joyously

♦ Encourage risk taking by making it safe for others to express their concerns freely

◆ Conduct weekly meetings to share accomplishments, challenges, and future direction

◆ Place team members into positions of leadership by allowing them to lead staff meeting segments and propose solutions to current challenges

◆ Look for opportunities to cross-train and job-shadow to strengthen team flexibility

Senior Leader Goals

◆ Create a work environment where employees can motivate themselves

◆ Make integrity and authenticity the cornerstones of your leadership style

◆ Demonstrate appreciation and recognition for employees' efforts to go above and beyond the call of duty

◆ Make sure that pay-for-performance is the primary driver of your team's success

◆ Model and encourage an appropriate work-life balance

◆ Foster a greater sense of community and inclusion

◆ Build career progression plans to grow and retain top talent

◆ Encourage philanthropic and voluntary activities to help the community

◆ Lead from your heart so that others will willingly follow you wherever you lead them

◆ Constantly share the bigger picture, and allow staffers to peer into your world, your concerns, and your larger overall goals

◆ Model your corporate values at all times

◆ Stimulate greater employee engagement by strengthening the quality of people leadership in your area

◆ Build a culture based on trust, open communication, recognition, and high expectations

◆ Institute the appropriate recognition and rewards programs to motivate top performers

◆ Inspire company loyalty by sharing the vision of its future growth

Oral and Written Expression

Early Career Goals

♦ Realize that others place more value on the insightfulness of your questions than on the depth of your statements

♦ Clearly demonstrate a mastery of basic business writing techniques

♦ Structure your key ideas into no more than three bullets per e-mail

♦ Consistently use the spelling and grammar check feature before sending an e-mail

♦ Avoid emoticons like smiley faces and instant messaging shorthand that others may not understand (e.g., LOL)

♦ Don't let grammar or usage errors distract from your message or from others' impression of you

♦ Reread all correspondence to ensure clarity before clicking the Send button

♦ Avoid any perception of plagiarism by quoting sources accurately

♦ Use simple language and delete words, sentences, or phrases that detract from your message

♦ Learn to say no respectfully but firmly

♦ Write in a natural and conversational tone

♦ Master grammar essentials by distinguishing between commonly misused words like "effect/affect," "insure/ensure," "it's/its," "accept/except," and "who/whom"

Administration/Operational Support Goals

♦ Focus on constructing correspondence that is brief, cogent, and error free

- Allow lots of white space on the page to ensure that the form of your communication complements the simplicity of your content
- Write the conclusion of your message or your recommendation in the Subject line at the top of an e-mail
- Include only those who have a need to know in your e-mail distribution chain
- Avoid vague words or jargon that will leave your audience guessing as to your intent
- Avoid the chained-elephant syndrome of rocking back and forth in one place when you present in public by planting your feet firmly and locking eye contact with an attentive member of the audience
- When in doubt, don't capitalize (for example, with titles and names of departments)
- Avoid sarcasm in both your oral and written presentations
- Use wide margins to aid readability
- Recast a sentence to avoid any inadvertent sexist references (e.g., using terms like chairman versus chair, fireman versus firefighter, and housewife versus homemaker)

Individual Contributor Goals

- Look for ways to feel more at ease when addressing large audiences
- Avoid interrupting others by counting to two before responding
- Use active eye contact to ensure that the listener knows that you understand
- Construct logical arguments by mapping out your key message points in advance
- Avoid overthinking or overanalyzing your narrative drafts
- Construct logical paragraphs that organize the content of your message
- Be careful not to let excessive narratives distract from your written message
- Use high-resolution, 300+-dpi TIF files for electronic photos
- Stress benefits rather than features to persuade your audience
- Prefer informal to formal language in your writing
- Ensure that your writing remains relaxed, informal, and friendly by using contractions to warm up your message

Front-Line Supervisory and Managerial Goals

♦ Don't "shout" when you write by using too many exclamation points or by writing in all caps

♦ Realize that the *e* in e-mail stands for "evidence," and don't commit anything to an electronic record that you wouldn't expect to see on the cover of *The New York Times*

♦ Improve your grammar skills by referencing Strunk & White's *The Elements of Style*, Blake & Bly's *The Elements of Business Writing*, or another standard stylebook

♦ Practice and time your presentation to avoid speaking too quickly

♦ Adjust the language of your presentation to fit the audience's tastes

♦ Avoid wordy and redundant phrases

♦ Encourage others by turning "yes . . . *but*" into "yes . . . *and*" statements

Senior Leader Goals

♦ Use an executive summary to highlight the critical aspects of your message

♦ Write to express, not to impress

♦ Avoid drafting memos that are longer than one page

♦ Write in a natural and conversational style

♦ Avoid excessive verbiage like "leverage economies of scale for optimal efficiencies" or "encourage holistic talent building," which only confuses your audience

♦ Focus on developing the *gravitas* to hold a room and command respect

♦ Employ the attorney-client privilege by copying your attorney, asking for a legal analysis and opinion, and limiting your audience to as few individuals as possible

♦ Avoid metaphors and idioms that are difficult to translate into a foreign language

♦ Use contractions whenever possible to personalize your message

♦ Draft reports using the following subheading structure: executive summary, background, findings, conclusions, and recommendations

Organization and Planning Skills

Early Career Goals

♦ Plan your work, and work your plan

♦ Be careful to not overcommit your time or spread yourself too thin

♦ Fail to plan, plan to fail

♦ Appreciate the critical nature of well-honed organizational and planning skills

♦ Avoid any perception of being a seat-of-your-pants, reactive performer

♦ Rely on your daily planner to divide your day into blocks of productive time

♦ Maintain a workspace that is free from clutter and well organized

Administration/Operational Support Goals

♦ Tie up loose ends before moving on to other projects

♦ Rank potential problems according to their likelihood of occurrence, and prepare contingency plans in advance accordingly

♦ Ensure that you can access and pull backup data quickly and consistently

♦ Manage multiple projects on parallel tracks more effectively by assigning specific responsibilities and deliverables to key individuals

♦ Avoid appearing overwhelmed by multiple priorities or pending deadlines

- Employ an Excel spreadsheet to track all incoming calls to ensure that you never lose callers' historical contact data
- File documents immediately upon receipt
- Don't get discouraged by unexpected delays, and see them as opportunities to demonstrate your preparedness and flexibility

Individual Contributor Goals

- Identify project stakeholders, and keep them abreast of all ongoing communications
- Employ a flowcharting software program to create a master plan and track incremental progress
- Ensure that other team members can easily replicate repetitive tasks in your absence
- Be careful not to appear overly reliant on rules, policies, or other fixed guidelines that limit flexibility and responsiveness
- Demonstrate a methodical, consistent, and reliable approach when organizing your work
- Rely on your years of service to "trend out" and prepare for seasonal spikes in volume
- Readily adhere to deadlines and production benchmarks
- Become your department's divining rod in sniffing out periods of peak productivity due to potential customer demand
- Don't allow productivity to wane as the number of simultaneous activities increases

Front-Line Supervisory and Managerial Goals

- Delegate wisely by sharing both control and authority in getting things done
- Delegate according to others' strengths and interests
- Pay special attention to any weak links in the delivery process
- Don't be afraid to work through others whom you may not directly supervise

♦ Set up projects for success by clearly communicating your end goal, incremental steps and mileposts, and the concrete and measurable outcomes necessary for completion

♦ Sensitize your team members to use what-if scenarios to forecast potential problems

♦ Keep it simple, and don't get lost in a myriad of details

♦ Demonstrate the appropriate amount of patience, flexibility, and wise guidance in helping others manage projects through to completion

Senior Leader Goals

♦ Effectively translate theoretical ideas into concrete, tactical action plans

♦ Focus on the 80–20 principle, where the top 20% of your employees generates 80% of the work

♦ Budget reserves in cases of cost overruns or unforeseen delays

♦ Delegate as a means of growing and developing your staff

♦ Identify up front the appropriate resources that you'll need in terms of people, budgets, funding, materials, and other support

♦ Conduct a more thorough needs assessment in the preplanning stage of project management

♦ Strengthen your organizational forecasting ability by anticipating bottlenecks, problems, and pitfalls

♦ Avoid any perception of perpetuating a management-by-crisis leadership style

♦ Hold yourself accountable for getting things done both through the company's formal channels and informal networks

♦ Propose concrete and definitive strategies and tactics

♦ Distinguish between and prioritize strategic and tactical goals

♦ Orchestrate an ensemble of functional areas by designating key leads for each area of responsibility

Personal Style

Early Career Goals

♦ Readily assume responsibility for things gone wrong

♦ Always remain open to and encourage constructive criticism

♦ Constantly look for opportunities to assume responsibilities beyond your job description

♦ Ask insightful and penetrating questions, not questions for questions' sake

♦ Reinvent yourself in light of your department's changing needs

♦ Look for new ways of adding value to your role over time

♦ Always show a can-do attitude and a high level of enthusiasm and self-confidence

♦ Acknowledge your own shortcomings rather than appear to be defensive

♦ Discipline yourself to plan more effectively rather than fly by the seat of your pants

Administration/Operational Support Goals

♦ Avoid procrastinating by breaking tasks down into manageable segments

♦ Build strong, supportive, and constructive relationships with your peers

♦ Become more comfortable working with "fuzzy edges" where every *i* may not be dotted and every *t* may not be crossed

♦ Overcome your natural risk averseness by aiming for small wins

- Strengthen your capacity for analytical thinking and problem solving
- Handle interruptions, breaks in routine, and last-minute changes without breaking stride
- Practice multitasking rather than performing one task at a time
- Hone your listening skills by not interrupting others and using eye contact to demonstrate your understanding and to connect with the speaker
- Minimize the impact of outside influences on your job performance
- Don't simply roll over and maintain amicable relations at all costs
- Respect both the letter and the spirit of company policies
- Look to find equilibrium between your high-volume production and quality ratios
- Avoid using sarcasm or offensive humor that may appear to put down others in the organization
- Balance your career with your personal life more effectively
- Exemplify commitment, discipline, and a solid work ethic in all you do
- Strengthen your organizational forecasting abilities in terms of predicting needs before they arise
- Rely less on your engaging personality and more on producing substantive work

Individual Contributor Goals

- Remain sensitive to others' needs
- Assume good intentions unless and until proven otherwise
- Be careful not to get mired in minutia and tedious detail
- Find new ways to build your individual energy level and capacity for hustle
- Accept that others are not responsible for accommodating your mood swings or inappropriate language; instead, you are responsible for accommodating theirs
- Never leave your supervisor feeling as if he or she is flying blind or not in the know
- Use diplomacy and tact when working with peers and customers alike

◆ Strengthen your commitment to project completion

◆ See how things *can* be done rather than why they can't be done

◆ Demonstrate a greater tolerance for dealing with your department's shortcomings

◆ Become more effective at managing others' expectations

Front-Line Supervisory and Managerial Goals

◆ Encourage brainstorming to minimize analysis paralysis

◆ Bolster your self-confidence by focusing on your strengths and positive relationships

◆ Never delay the inevitable disciplining or dismissal of employees

◆ Avoid getting personally involved in others' conflicts

◆ Stay open to all sides of an argument before reaching a decision

◆ Provide greater structure, direction, and feedback to your team

◆ Praise in public, censure in private

◆ Encourage your team to work more autonomously and independently

◆ Avoid developing a reputation as someone who takes action without getting prior approval

◆ Create ways for your team to feed information up to you more effectively

◆ Analyze successes and failures openly for clues to improvement

◆ When managing staff, *inspect* more than you *expect*

◆ Build stronger teams to give your company a key competitive advantage

◆ Practice MBWA (management by walking around) to better control your team and to keep abreast of what's going on

◆ Become more proficient in the use of new technology

Senior Leader Goals

◆ When in doubt, always err on the side of compassion

◆ Demonstrate the highest level of ethics and values at all times

- Abide by the terms of business conduct as outlined in the company's code of conduct
- Readily share the wealth of your institutional knowledge
- Create an environment where people can motivate themselves
- Pick up on social clues, and learn to read people more accurately
- Learn to cope more effectively with the significant pressures associated with senior management
- Transition from an autocratic to a more consensus-building and participative leadership style
- View yourself as a facilitator of progressive change within the organization
- Practice turnaround leadership, where you salvage problem units suffering from low productivity or poor morale
- Create a culture of open information sharing and increased accountability
- Look for creative ways of turning theoretical vision into workable practice

Problem-Solving Skills and Results Orientation

Early Career Goals

♦ Learn to break down problems into their component parts

♦ Ask more clarifying questions, but be careful to avoid asking repetitive questions that have already been addressed

♦ Use checklists regularly to ensure that you're consistently covering all the basics

♦ Don't sacrifice speed in solving problems by being overly methodical or risk averse

♦ Become more effective at recognizing repetitive trends in recurring problems

♦ Look for small and incremental wins when challenged by larger problems

♦ Differentiate yourself from your peers by focusing on achievements and acquiring best-practice principles along the way

♦ Always welcome creative suggestions from others

♦ View impediments as solvable challenges

Administration/Operational Support Goals

♦ Work through ambiguity and chaos, keeping your eye on the end goal

♦ Be careful not to appear to use only old solutions to new problems

♦ Readily distinguish between core causes and secondary symptoms of problems

♦ Turn a problem upside down, and look at its mirror image to find new solutions

- Look for parallels, patterns, and precedence when approaching new problems for the first time
- Brainstorm, combine, and clarify nascent ideas—without judgment or criticism

Individual Contributor Goals

- Break complex projects down into their simple component parts
- When facing an analysis-paralysis challenge, do what authors do to avoid writers' block: put your ideas down on paper without judging them
- Always look to the bigger picture of why something needs to be done, and determine the shortest way of getting there
- Organize your office more efficiently so that you can readily tap historical data
- Avoid having to master every detail at every stage of the process; a perfectionist approach will likely slow you down
- When prodding groups for creative solutions, freedom of ideas comes first, structure comes second

Front-Line Supervisory and Managerial Goals

- Be careful to avoid developing a perception as a fire-ready-aim type of leader
- Provide the appropriate amount of structure and direction to your team to help them solve problems and anticipate change
- Develop a quarterly achievement calendar on your computer share drive so that all team members have access and can update their projects and accomplishments
- Discipline your team to provide three solutions for every challenge they face
- Avoid your penchant for making fault-free decisions and minimizing risk and criticism
- Make it safe to experiment and learn in your department, as if it were a laboratory dedicated to solving problems

♦ Address problem issues head-on in a proactive fashion

♦ Ask more questions to help employees rethink and reframe the problem to generate multiple solutions

♦ Don't oversimplify and choke off alternatives too early in the problem-solving process

Senior Leader Goals

♦ Help your group leaders add bullets of accomplishments to both their resumes and their year-end self-evaluations to develop more of an achievement mentality

♦ Don't be so results driven that you fail to properly define the initial problem

♦ See visionary leadership through creative problem solving as your primary responsibility within your company

♦ Focus your department heads on doing the right things, not just doing things right

♦ Avoid sharp reactions that can stifle risk taking and thinking outside the box

♦ Involve diverse groups from different functions, levels, and disciplines to brainstorm and generate ideas in a stream-of-conscience manner

♦ Understand that, if your people aren't making mistakes, they're not stretching the rubber band enough

Productivity and Volume

Early Career Goals

- Look always to collaborate, organize, prioritize, simplify, and reinforce
- Focus on improving your personal productivity to create higher value results
- Question always, "What are the things that keep me from performing at my best?"
- Develop and strengthen your creative problem-solving abilities, including goal setting and influencing skills
- Look always to see how you can help others to build credibility and goodwill across borders and boundaries
- Set mini project deadlines for yourself to monitor your own progress
- Avoid becoming too dependent on yourself
- Overcome internal barriers to productivity
- Plan your work, and work your plan

Administration/Operational Support Goals

- Create greater results in less time
- Balance multitasking with unitasking to ensure that you complete what you start
- Minimize disruptions from normal daily activity
- Commit to the quality and accuracy aspects of your work, and allow volume to catch up over time
- Focus less on dotting every *i* and crossing every *t* so that you won't be slowed down and can meet your volume benchmarks

◆ When working at your desk, log off from your e-mail and forward your phone to voice mail for 30 minutes to allow for uninterrupted concentration

Individual Contributor Goals

◆ Avoiding becoming infatuated with marginally productive ideas

◆ Focus on achieving the maximum result for the least effort and the largest output from the smallest input

◆ Integrate product development and process improvement with the company's value-chain strategy

◆ Determine how best to meet technology challenges, from R&D to manufacturing and from project management to engineering

◆ Figure out what you're worth per hour by adding your gross salary plus benefits and overhead to attach a monetary value to your time

◆ Establish a funding time line to track ongoing expenditures against plan

◆ Regularly provide progress feedback up to your supervisor via e-mail

◆ Create efficient workflows and processes

Front-Line Supervisory and Managerial Goals

◆ Ensure that your employees know how you judge and measure their performance

◆ Encourage individual development with training and educational programs

◆ Ensure that you understand how your employees' time is spent

◆ Provide timely, accurate, and open two-way communication with your employees

◆ Provide objective job performance standards with timely feedback

◆ Turn ideas into action, put creativity to work, and develop strategies for innovation

◆ Transform your culture by delegating, empowering, and sharing credit

◆ Set mission-critical priorities, and avoid getting diverted by trivia

◆ Design workflows and processes that maximize productivity without leading to burnout

◆ Increase your number of misfires and mistakes by pushing the envelope and taking more risks

◆ Assume responsibility for things gone wrong, while always sharing credit for things gone right

Senior Leader Goals

◆ Focus on increasing worker motivation and satisfaction to increase worker output

◆ Create a culture of flexible, diverse work assignments, allowing for self-regulation, variety, and challenge

◆ Get higher-quality job performance from your employees by giving them opportunities for personal growth, achievement, responsibility, recognition, and reward

◆ Strengthen your ability to respond to the demands of the ever changing marketplace

◆ Create new and more effective ways of adding value to customers

◆ Continuously manage the effect of external changes on your employees and ultimately employee motivation and performance

◆ See our employees as the intellectual capital that gives our company its competitive edge

◆ Provide your department with a strategic road map for creativity, problem solving, innovation, and transformation

◆ Use training opportunities to develop creative people, innovative teams, and profitable revenue streams

◆ Recognize that proper delegation, communication, and the setting of priorities and goals will help employees feel empowered and motivated

Professionalism and Grooming/Appearance

Early Career Goals

♦ Dress for the interview, not for the job

♦ Realize that you have only one chance to make a first impression

♦ Focus on grooming and appearance standards as an opportunity to stand out as a rarity among your peers

♦ Look always to project a positive self-image

♦ View yourself as the ultimate representative of your company in all you do

♦ Arrive at work fully dressed with your hair done and makeup already on

♦ Treat others with dignity and respect at all times

♦ Understand that good manners are always the very best place to start

♦ Work smarter, not harder

Administration/Operational Support Goals

♦ Demonstrate a fresh, crisp, and clean look in your daily attire

♦ Always exude self-confidence and inspire confidence in others

♦ Remain a source of calmness and focus in high-stress situations

♦ Model best practices in all you do

♦ Never engage in thoughtless gossip or appear to feed the corporate grapevine

♦ Consistently meet all personal hygiene standards without exception

♦ Avoid any perceptions of having "too many wears before a wash" when it comes to your own personal dress code

♦ Dress the part to create an initial impression of success

♦ Don't procrastinate; set tight deadlines for yourself and prioritize your workload

Individual Contributor Goals

♦ Differentiate how you dress on days when customers will visit the back office

♦ Use the appropriate amount of discretion when it comes to revealing tattoos, body piercings, or jewelry choices

♦ Maintain confidentiality and respect for others' private affairs

♦ Consistently walk the talk by modeling appropriate workplace behaviors

♦ Welcome constructive feedback from peers and staff alike

♦ Avoid topics relating to politics, religion, or late-night TV that may easily antagonize others or instigate feelings of resentment

♦ Eliminate from your vocabulary any utterances of "how stupid this company is," "how many people around here are idiots," or similar negative judgments

♦ Know that grooming and appearance are not hit-or-miss standards, and dress appropriately every day without exception

♦ Remove or cover potentially offensive body piercings when dealing with customers

Front-Line Supervisory and Managerial Goals

♦ Model your company's standards for appropriate dress and professionalism

♦ Avoid using inappropriate jargon or idioms

♦ Ensure that all team members wear the appropriate uniform insignia at all times

♦ Consistently follow up with subordinates in a timely fashion

♦ Explain why something can't be done rather than simply saying no

- Avoid any perceptions of your throwing others under the bus or placing blame elsewhere
- Share credit generously
- Establish and model productive work habits for your team
- Eliminate profanity from your vocabulary
- Avoid interrupting or talking over others

Senior Leader Goals

- Consistently enforce proper hygiene standards at the plant
- Enforce all uniform standards to minimize the possibility of workers wearing union pins or buttons in an attempt to organize
- Enforce the mandatory hardhat rule for all visiting guests
- Look to the policy and procedure manual as well as to the company's code of conduct to avoid any perception of a conflict of interest
- Consistently enforce company policy, and act within established guidelines
- Foster a more inclusive and positive work environment
- Project an image of professionalism that others can model and follow
- Ensure that all employees are aware of your company's mission statement
- Always justify exceptions to policies and past practices
- When in doubt, ask; begging for exceptions after the fact is not a suitable alternative
- Look for new ways of establishing *gravitas* and holding a room when presenting in public

Quality

Early Career Goals

♦ Strive always for maximum effectiveness and efficiency

♦ Refuse to sacrifice quality for volume

♦ Recognize that rework is much more expensive than getting it right the first time

♦ Plan your work, and work your plan

♦ Anticipate problems before they occur

♦ Offer two solutions for every challenge that you encounter

♦ Ask quality questions, but avoid repetition of common things you should know

♦ Find an appropriate balance between quality and quantity

♦ Demonstrate best practices in all that you do

Administration/Operational Support Goals

♦ Avoid delays and cost overruns by underpromising and overdelivering

♦ Plan your resources and time lines before committing to a deadline

♦ Identify streamlining measures that eliminate or reduce system redundancies

♦ Quantify budget elements such as wages, funding, tools, and materials before you begin a new project

♦ Consistently dot your *i*'s and cross your *t*'s

♦ Gain appropriate budget signoff before making commitments to others

◆ Consistently rely on your computer's spell-check feature before e-mailing

◆ Reread any and all proposed correspondence for grammar and syntax accuracy

◆ Take notes and write down instructions in order to replicate results in the future

◆ Write e-mails as if every message was going to be blown up on the cover page of *The New York Times*

◆ Implement measurement tools that increase efficiency and reduce costs

Individual Contributor Goals

◆ Establish yardsticks for continuous improvement

◆ Remain customer oriented, flexible, and responsive

◆ Employ sequencing and flowchart software to anticipate roadblocks

◆ Nurture your network of industry experts and peers as a reliable resource to turn to when brainstorming about trends among the competition

◆ Accept that perfectionism isn't necessary in an industry driven by time-to-market

◆ Look always to surprise your customers with unanticipated benefits, including lower costs and shortened delivery timeframes

◆ Avoid implementing unreasonable quality standards that cause unnecessary delays

◆ Produce a work product reasonably free from errors, waste, and rework

◆ Lower your scrap rate to acceptable company standards

Front-Line Supervisory and Managerial Goals

◆ Set clear goals and objectives, along with intermittent follow-up points

◆ Be patient enough to explore second and third iterations of proposed solutions

- Document the measures of quality and high performance that you expect
- Focus your team on not getting bogged down in analysis paralysis
- Don't allow error rates to exceed acceptable thresholds
- Conduct ongoing self-audits to ensure maximum efficiency
- Teach team members to rely more on documentation than on their memories
- Encourage all team members to pursue appropriate licenses, certifications, and accreditation
- Address substandard work quality issues directly and in a timely manner

Senior Leader Goals

- Benchmark best practices by looking to industry trade associations and agencies
- Research your competitors' products and services in order to differentiate your organization's uniqueness
- Create internal competitions between two teams tasked with identifying viable solutions to ongoing quality challenges
- Implement quality assurance standards to maximize effectiveness and efficiency
- Publicize the link between higher-quality standards and increased customer retention
- Equate higher-quality leadership with greater employee retention and engagement
- Employ metrics and analytics to track and trend customer feedback regarding product quality and reliability
- Actively identify trends and patterns in client turnover
- Institute a quality training program that allows recent graduates to bridge the transition from academia to the workplace
- View quality as the single most essential element that allows our company to compete effectively and to differentiate itself from the competition

Safety

Early Career Goals

♦ Adhere to all company safety and security policy regulations

♦ Ensure that your equipment is in proper working order before initiating work

♦ Always leave your work area clean and functional at the end of your shift

♦ Maintain your personal tools in proper working order

♦ Familiarize yourself with all safety instruments and resources

♦ Maintain a personal safety record beyond reproach

♦ Return all tools to their proper place when no longer in use

Administration/Operational Support Goals

♦ Report potential safety hazards immediately

♦ Maintain all machinery in compliance with safety manual guidelines

♦ Maintain all equipment according to manufacturers' specifications

♦ Communicate any potential malfunctioning equipment at shift change

♦ Monitor visitors, suppliers, and vendors to ensure safety in the workplace

♦ Remedy any violations identified during the internal audit process before they are discovered by outside inspectors

♦ Develop a formal response plan for audits, inspections, and investigations

♦ Post all workers' comp notices in compliance with government regulations

- Implement measures to eliminate or mitigate employee exposure to workplace health hazards
- Stringently follow all injury and illness reporting and record keeping requirements

Individual Contributor Goals

- Always wear the appropriate safety gear on the shop floor
- Cooperate with safety investigations and audit requests
- Remain informed about how to identify known hazards and neutralize their dangers
- Maintain required licenses and certifications in good order
- Never sacrifice safety for productivity
- Comply with all safety recommendations, postings, and requirements
- Recommend effective safety enhancements and corrective actions
- Understand the hazards and the rules for working safely with machinery

Front-Line Supervisory and Managerial Goals

- Minimize workplace injury and illness occurrences
- Track and trend changes in worker injury rates
- Only permit fully trained employees to operate new machinery
- Request an ergonomic assessment of your work area
- Stringently follow all recommendations outlined in material safety data sheets
- Follow up immediately on any reports of pending hazards
- Insist on a zero tolerance policy for safety infractions
- Discipline workers who fail to adhere to company safety standards
- Communicate emergency evacuation procedures during new hire orientation
- Ensure that team members consistently adhere to environmental safety and health practices

♦ Maintain all OSHA housekeeping rules regarding a clean and sanitary workplace

Senior Leader Goals

♦ Continuously evaluate best practices in environmental and safety procedures

♦ Establish a workplace safety and health committee

♦ Manage the business continuity planning and disaster recovery programs

♦ Make a compelling business case for implementing an EHS (environmental health and safety) program by translating initiatives into bottom-line results

♦ Report enterprise-wide safety concerns to local authorities

♦ Identify major equipment replacements that will come due over the next 18 months

♦ Strictly enforce all environmental regulations

♦ Implement an equipment maintenance improvement strategy that will minimize unplanned failures

♦ Regularly publicize available safety awards and incentives

♦ Establish a relationship with an outside security firm in case violence in the workplace ever becomes an issue

♦ Lead disaster drills and emergency evacuation planning exercises

♦ Establish documented maintenance schedules for major equipment to ensure minimal downtime or delays

♦ Coordinate emergency drills with the local fire department

♦ Schedule and oversee third-party inspections of plant machinery to comply with government certification requirements

Self-Development

Early Career Goals

♦ Look for opportunities to assume greater responsibilities

♦ Identify the future career path of your current position

♦ Research the dominant and growth-oriented companies in your industry in order to know the key players

♦ Always assume responsibility for a problem, and see yourself as part of the solution

♦ Focus on your career rather than on your job

♦ Expect to kiss some frogs before you find your prince

♦ Study and share best practices

♦ Ask insightful questions that add value to group discussions

♦ Set realistic and concrete goals

♦ Align yourself with leaders who naturally mentor, grow, and develop their teams

♦ Join alliance or affinity groups where you have things in common with peers

♦ Train yourself to provide two solutions for each question you raise

Administration/Operational Support Goals

♦ Seek a healthy work-life balance

♦ Master the art of successful negotiation

♦ Focus more on relationship and less on transaction

♦ Set the highest expectations for yourself in terms of ethics and integrity

♦ Be willing to share negative news promptly and directly

♦ Engage in positive confrontation rather than avoidance

♦ Keep your personal opinions to yourself and restrict conversations to work-related topics

♦ Always look for opportunities to reinvent the workflow in light of our department's changing needs

♦ Focus on making bad relationships good and good relationships better

Individual Contributor Goals

♦ Determine your year-end goals and the measurable outcomes that will demonstrate that you've reached them

♦ Identify two or three skills to build your resume and create a plan to achieve them

♦ Research offsite workshops to build your financial knowledge

♦ Consider whether you want to pursue a technical or managerial career track

♦ Read our company's 10(k) report to familiarize yourself with the key financial drivers of organizational success

♦ Purchase and read a book on nonprofit law and governance

♦ Take advantage of your company's e-learning offerings

♦ Use your company's tuition reimbursement benefit to pursue your professional designation in HR

♦ Draft your self-evaluation focusing on specific achievements and accomplishments that have increased revenues, decreased costs, or saved time

♦ Search out opportunities to give back to the community

♦ Be cautious of overusing sarcastic humor to prove a point

♦ Heed Mark Twain's adage, "If we were meant to talk more than we listen, we would have two mouths and one ear"

Front-Line Supervisory and Managerial Goals

♦ See what's so; do what works

- Motivation is internal, and your job is to create an environment where others can motivate themselves
- Avoid any perceptions of drama or histrionics when dealing with conflict
- See yourself as a role model who embodies the company's mission and values
- Ensure that your reputation for fairness is beyond reproach
- You have every right to observe objectively, but avoid any semblance of judging others
- Find creative ways to surprise your staff
- Look for signs of an overreactive grapevine as evidence of staff discontent
- Never promise confidentiality before knowing the nature of the question or request
- Always separate the people from the problem, and assume good intentions
- Debrief regularly and elicit ongoing feedback
- Foster a sense of engagement and involvement in all that you do

Senior Leader Goals

- Teach what you choose to learn
- Recognize that perception is reality until proven otherwise; therefore, always hold yourself accountable for your own perception management
- Employ right-brain imagination, artistry, and intuition, along with left-brain logic and planning
- Nix conversations about politics, religion, or other politically incorrect nonwork-related issues that are sure to foster resentments or frustration
- When in doubt, keep it simple
- Avoid overthinking problems and look for simple and straightforward solutions
- Sell your ideas enthusiastically, but avoid looking like you're railroading others
- Remain open to constructive criticism

- Realize that no one does anything wrong given his or her model of the world; therefore, when dealing with hurt feelings or long-term resentments among staffers, look for common interests and underlying concerns to heal a wound in the group

- Set the tone, and model the behaviors that encourage openness and transparency

- When in doubt, always err on the side of compassion

Staff Development

Early Career Goals

♦ *Not applicable*

Administration/Operational Support Goals

♦ Follow the simple adage, "What you want for yourself, give to another"

♦ Actively rotate assignments to ensure cross-functional capabilities within the team

♦ Define your current leadership style against the way you'd ideally like to be described by your team members

♦ Raise your awareness level of your natural tendency to overly defend yourself or to place blame elsewhere

♦ Be a resource to peers and associates in order to help them achieve their goals

♦ Promote the benefits of a diverse workforce

♦ Put others' needs ahead of your own, and expect them to respond in kind

♦ Encourage individuality, and foster an environment of respect and inclusion

♦ Learn what you can change about your own behavior to invoke a different response from others

♦ Encourage others to engage in random acts of kindness

Individual Contributor Goals

♦ *Not applicable*

Front-Line Supervisory and Managerial Goals

- Praise in public, censure in private
- Practice selfless leadership
- Delegate what you're best at and what you enjoy in order to mentor others by sharing your strengths
- Get to know your team members better by learning two to three personal items per person (for example, hobbies, interests, children, education, vacation destinations, and the like)
- Refrain from providing immediate answers, and encourage your staffers to think things through with you logically and out loud
- Provide the appropriate amount of structure, direction, and feedback without handholding
- Encourage cross-training and job-shadowing to broaden your team's breadth and depth of skills and organizational knowledge
- Assign each team member a copy of your company's annual report and ensure that everyone understands the financial drivers of organizational success
- Create a book-of-the-quarter club, asking individual team members to identify practical applications in the workplace that they learn from their reading
- Avoid any perception of playing favorites or singling out individuals for scrutiny
- Welcome and encourage feedback
- Ensure that team members are comfortable sharing minor concerns with you before they become major impediments
- Convert "yes . . . *but*" to "yes . . . *and*" statements to acknowledge the speaker's point of view and to encourage additional insights

Senior Leader Goals

- Rotate leadership assignments to build staff members' confidence in managing projects from start to finish
- Articulate your game plan and end goals properly, and allow your employees to execute in the direction of a defined outcome
- Create a work environment where team members can motivate themselves

- Identify your successor
- Provide ongoing career guidance and coaching to your staff
- Help your subordinates prepare for their next move in career progression, whether at your company or elsewhere
- Ensure that subordinates understand their limits and boundaries
- Understand that beingness trumps doingness; focus more on who you are as a person and a leader rather than what you're doing at any given point in time
- Emphasize the qualities and activities associated with success rather than just end results
- Be cautious of your natural ability to instill fear in others, and avoid intimidation
- Remain conscious and aware of your natural tendency to interrupt, talk over others, or come across as a bull in a China closet
- Help your team find individual and creative solutions by asking, "I realize you don't know, but *if you did know*, what would your recommendation be?"
- Convince team members not to act on principle to the extent that rigid and self-justified positions allow for little compromise
- Ensure that your team communicates upward and asks for advanced permission rather than forgiveness afterward
- Above all, teach your employees appreciation and gratitude

Strategic and Critical Thinking Skills

Early Career Goals

♦ *Not applicable*

Administration/Operational Support Goals

♦ Identify unique ways of creating value
♦ Identify the key business drivers that differentiate your company from the competition
♦ Thoroughly research your options in terms of risks and consequences
♦ Combine your natural curiosity and gut intuition with sound analytical reasoning skills
♦ Think through the consequences of your recommended courses of action
♦ Assess in advance the benefits and consequences of your recommendations
♦ Use forecasts and models to project budget variances and cost overruns
♦ Strive to become a subject matter expert in your field
♦ Understand how your company makes and spends money by studying the annual report
♦ Strategically partner with your clients and present your recommendations on a problem-to-solution basis

Individual Contributor Goals

♦ Employ metrics and analytics to identify future trends and patterns

♦ Think always in terms of what-if scenarios that will help you ask the right questions in defining future growth plans

♦ Avoid jargon and buzzwords that amount to corporate-speak when simpler vocabulary will do

♦ Develop broader, deep-dive experience into your field by studying the competition

♦ Keep the pipeline of innovation open by driving research and development efforts to bring new products to market

♦ Don't be afraid to take risks or step outside your comfort zone: simply communicate your intended plan of action first so that your supervisor can provide guidance

♦ Embrace new technology and look for new approaches to increase efficiency

♦ Look for new ways of reinventing yourself in light of your company's changing needs

Front-Line Supervisory and Managerial Goals

♦ Encourage your staffers to think through larger trends that affect demand for your product

♦ Make it safe for team members to employ their curiosity and imagination

♦ Train others to think long term

♦ Help your team focus beyond the tactical here and now

♦ Research our top competitors' annual reports to anticipate future consequences and trends

♦ Employ a SWOT (strengths, weaknesses, opportunities, and threats) analysis format to project visions of possibilities and likelihoods

♦ Encourage team members who normally avoid risk or dislike uncertainty to volunteer subjective estimates of where your company and industry are heading

♦ Constantly prepare your people and your organization for change

♦ Encourage team members to take appropriate risks and embrace change

Senior Leader Goals

- ◆ Anticipate future business trends and industry progressions to continuously grow market share
- ◆ Strengthen your vocabulary by adding strategic buzzwords and terms
- ◆ Combine strategic and tactical thinking to address current and future business needs
- ◆ Avoid analysis paralysis by overcomplicating things or remaining too theoretical
- ◆ Encourage curiosity and imagination when employing what-if scenarios
- ◆ Develop strategic plans that recommend how best to deploy corporate resources
- ◆ Delegate tactical day-to-day responsibilities to free yourself up for long-term projection exercises
- ◆ Translate strategies into objectives and action plans
- ◆ Construct plausible future business scenarios and projections for your primary and secondary product lines
- ◆ Develop strategies that reflect your changing business priorities
- ◆ Make appropriate risk assumptions after analyzing the newest technology
- ◆ Use predictive analytics to forecast next-generation business needs
- ◆ Understand that being strategic requires a broader perspective, including knowledge of markets, budgets, and human capital
- ◆ Analyze industries and competitors to secure competitive advantage
- ◆ Unleash your corporate imagination
- ◆ Develop and own your organization's strategic business intelligence
- ◆ Ask questions that challenge subordinates to think outside the box and to render longer-term projections
- ◆ Compare departmental performance to industry benchmarks
- ◆ Don't shy away from making subjective estimates and best guesses as long as you can make an appropriate business case for your recommendations
- ◆ Define and communicate the vision for your department
- ◆ See yourself as a visionary strategist and futurist
- ◆ Align your department's tactical metrics to the company's broader business and profitability goals

Supervision

Early Career Goals

♦ *Not applicable*

Administration/Operational Support Goals

♦ *Not applicable*

Individual Contributor Goals

♦ *Not applicable*

Front-Line Supervisory and Managerial Goals

Structuring Work Assignments and Delegation

♦ Provide the proper amount of ongoing structure, direction, and feedback

♦ Structure your projects and assignments with clear goals and measurable outcomes so that team members can creatively individualize solutions

♦ Ensure that your integrity and character remain above reproach

♦ Collect best-practice ideas from your team in terms of getting work done more effectively and efficiently

♦ Break a task down into its component parts, and sequence the steps to completion

- Measure success incrementally by eating the elephant one bite at a time
- Balance your high productivity output with the company's quality goals and guidelines
- Always ask for advance approval rather than forgiveness afterward
- Define, delegate, and direct work in a flexible manner
- Set realistic work demands and a fair distribution of assignments
- Expect the unexpected and adjust to change accordingly
- Create efficient workflow processes, assign tasks by talent and interest level, and allocate resources properly
- Set appropriate goals and measures in light of your budget and staffing constraints
- Recognize that no one understands the customers' needs greater than those in the trenches, so value your front-line employees as your primary resource for success
- Plan, prioritize, and execute according to your predefined strategy
- Avoid appearing inconsistent or vague by setting the rules as you go along
- Design feedback loops to ensure that all members of your team are kept informed of key changes and updates
- Ensure the highest safety standards at all times
- Demonstrate your company's mission, vision, and values in all that you do
- Know that as a leader, you're the first domino: If not you, who? If not now, when?
- Above all else, be consistent and fair, and avoid any perception of double standards
- Manage with a conscience and place integrity, ethics, and, trust above all else
- Don't worry so much about completing everything you start neatly and cleanly; the goal is to move projects forward incrementally and have multiple balls in the air
- Motivate team members by having them set their own stretch goals
- Create a work environment where people can motivate themselves
- Always look to monitor process, progress, and results

♦ Prioritize the team's workload by setting appropriate benchmarks and guideposts

♦ Establish higher expectations and refuse to settle for mediocre results

Communication

♦ Communicate, communicate, communicate

♦ Limit confidential information to only those who have a strict need to know

♦ Never delay the inevitable in terms of addressing problematic performance or conduct issues

♦ When in doubt, document

♦ Engage in tough conversations when necessary and confront minor issues early on before they become major impediments

♦ Share your concerns in a positive and constructive manner

♦ Don't shy away from sharing how things look from your vantage point or how others' behaviors make you feel

♦ Act quickly by escalating problematic performance issues to Human Resources' attention

♦ Praise in public, censure in private

♦ Employ a consensus-building rather than autocratic supervisory style

♦ Storyboard your ideas to explain your vision or strategy for completing tasks on time and under budget

♦ Make it safe for subordinates to disagree with you and offer alternative approaches

♦ Develop a stronger leadership presence and gravitas by strengthening your vocabulary and developing your public speaking skills

♦ Become the beacon that everyone looks to in a crisis

♦ The ends do not justify the means; ensure that successful performance work habits and behaviors always accompany bottom-line results

♦ Share credit willingly and publicly—and as often as you can

♦ Think of three characteristics that made your favorite supervisor in your career stand out, and emulate them

♦ Provide ongoing progress feedback as you go

♦ Understand that beingness trumps doingness; become a superstar supervisor by being and living your key values, and you'll then do the right things that spring from there

♦ Never leave your supervisor flying blind or wondering what he or she may be missing

Interpersonal Skills

♦ Go out of your way to put others at ease

♦ When in doubt, slow down; errors result from hasty decisions

♦ Avoid appearing to railroad others into following your directives by explaining your logic, inviting feedback, and asking for alternative ways of getting things done

♦ Accept that it's not up to others to accommodate your mood swings or to divine from your actions how you may be feeling at a particular moment

♦ Exercise a calming influence on others when faced with stress, anxiety, or frustration

♦ Recognize your penchant for perfectionism and risk avoidance, and compensate accordingly

♦ Avoid sharp reactions or appearing to wear your emotions on your sleeve

♦ Create an inclusive work environment where all feel welcome to share ideas and suggestions

♦ Concede small points so that others can win

♦ Be careful not to act on principle to the extent that you leave little room for disagreement, counterarguments, or debate

♦ Avoid any appearance of insensitivity, arrogance, or lack of concern

♦ Don't hold yourself accountable for being right all the time; your job is to solve problems *through* others, not necessarily *for* others

♦ Be creative in recognizing and rewarding good work

♦ When faced with disappointing news, ask, "Why is this happening *for* me?" rather than "Why is this happening *to* me?"

♦ Learn the rules of engagement in conducting corporate battle properly by aligning your resources in advance and gaining the appropriate guidance up front

♦ Inspire employees to take ownership of their performance improvement

♦ Familiarize yourself with the so-called hidden org chart before you negatively engage someone who's lower than you on the corporate totem pole

♦ Pick your battles wisely, and allow others to save face

♦ Practice *servant leadership* by placing others' needs ahead of your own and expecting them to respond in kind

Senior Leader Goals

♦ *Not applicable*

Teamwork and Relationship-Building Skills

Early Career Goals

♦ Place others' needs ahead of your own, and have the greater good in mind

♦ Always look to bring out the best in others

♦ Assume good intentions unless and until proven otherwise

♦ Listen actively, and always remain approachable and easy to do business with

♦ Actively cooperate, and explain the rationale for your recommendations

♦ Share best practices

♦ Consider the adage, "All the things that proceed *from* you return *to* you" (that is, "What goes around comes around")

♦ There is no "I" in "team"

Administration/Operational Support Goals

♦ Celebrate successes, and readily acknowledge your peers' efforts and achievements

♦ Create a common mindset of learning, growing, and acquiring new skills

♦ Limit sharing confidential information to build and maintain trust

♦ Keep conflicts small and see yourself as a peacemaker

♦ Bond normally conflicting departments by searching for common ground and shared understandings

- Look for opportunities to engage in the lateral exchange of information and resources
- Be careful not to judge other groups or to create impressions of superiority within your team

Individual Contributor Goals

- Avoid any appearance of withholding information or resources from your peer group
- Recognize that individual competition is healthy but, if taken to an extreme, may become detrimental to the overall group's efforts
- Look for common ground, and encourage collaboration with your peers
- Be careful not to demonstrate a cold, insensitive, or impersonal style or otherwise to put off others
- Always give others a chance to explain their side of the story before resorting to blame or assuming bad intentions
- Avoid any perception of preferring to be left alone to work solo
- Appreciate the variety of opinion that emanates from your peer group
- Recognize how groups can help people achieve their individual goals

Front-Line Supervisory and Managerial Goals

- Determine the motivational drivers of your team to help them build and grow their careers
- Share successes and use postmortems to learn and grow from failures
- Appreciate that each group will have its own personality and needs
- Capitalize on the talents of your team members
- Resolve team conflict without drama or angst
- Foster a sense of shared accountability and group responsibility
- Look to a group's collective power to accelerate solutions

♦ Be willing to negotiate, strike bargains, and establish reciprocity to harness the group's power

Senior Leader Goals

♦ Empower your team to embrace change opportunities

♦ Delegate to people's strengths to empower and enrich them

♦ Become a masterful facilitator of meaningful change

♦ Find creative ways of working toward consensus

♦ Internal teams are not supposed to be support groups where people with the same need join together to defend themselves from outward attack

♦ Raise your awareness regarding the impropriety of jokes or political comments made in front of mixed company

♦ View individual differences in opinion as value-adds to group thought

Technical Skills

Early Career Goals

♦ Benchmark best practices

♦ Strive always for continuous process improvement

♦ Constantly look for ways to strengthen your SKA (skills, knowledge, and abilities) in your chosen discipline

♦ Identify the critical technical skills that will help drive your career

♦ Be an early tester of new technology, and champion its introduction at work

♦ Look for opportunities to teach others in an effort to strengthen your understanding and conceptualization of emerging technologies

Administration/Operational Support Goals

♦ Dedicate yourself to honing your task, time, and computer skills

♦ Never underestimate the value of developing the soft skills of influencing and persuading others

♦ Carefully organize technical presentations for maximum comprehension

♦ Familiarize yourself quickly with your organization's technology, terminology, and technical challenges

♦ Avoid burnout from information overload by prioritizing your tasks and always looking to understand the bigger picture

♦ Leverage your advanced technical skills by creating metrics and analytics that drive your company's human capital strategy

♦ Develop a consistent methodology for diagnosing repetitive problems

Individual Contributor Goals

- Look for incremental changes, but be willing to start over and reengineer processes from scratch
- Venture beyond the confines of your academic discipline to explore and experiment freely
- Combine your technical skills with business acumen and a healthy dose of creativity to customize solutions for your clients
- Rely on cutting-edge technology as a tool to strengthen individual and group capacities and capabilities
- Develop apprentice relationships with earlier-career peers who can benefit from your deep-dive knowledge of emerging technology
- Actively search the Internet for product upgrades and security patches
- Maintain your technical and professional certifications

Front-Line Supervisory and Managerial Goals

- Create an environment of experimentation and healthy curiosity
- Solicit suggestions and feedback from subordinates, and make it safe to ask what-if questions
- Translate technical jargon into user-friendly information
- When dealing with specialized knowledge workers, always look to guide, rather than direct, team performance
- Equip your team members with the technical skills necessary to work confidently and independently
- Recognize that highly skilled, technical employees are often the most challenging to manage
- Ensure comprehension of new technical materials that may otherwise be considered dry or boring
- Don't get lost in techno-speak by employing arcane words or overly relying on industry-specific acronyms

Senior Leader Goals

- Balance your department's finely tuned technical skills with a broader, big-picture focus

- ◆ Recognize that many of your departmental leaders rose to management positions because of their exceptional technical expertise, not people skills, and accommodate accordingly
- ◆ Leverage your company's technical skills to strengthen our brand and drive business results
- ◆ Avoid any perception of being wed to past technologies or resistance to change
- ◆ Promote new technology as a way to increase efficiency and reduce costs
- ◆ Beware of the budget implications of introducing the newest technologies into your operation

Time Management

Early Career Goals

♦ Visualize your goals to ensure achievement

♦ Focus on maximizing your time in an effort to work smarter, not harder

♦ Write your goals down to make them tangible and to amplify and crystallize their importance

♦ Focus on building achievements and accomplishments into your resume and annual self-review as a guiding principal of your own career development

♦ Label priorities from A to F to help you focus on high-payoff activities

♦ Frame your goals as positive and encouraging statements to motivate yourself

♦ Review and update your to-do list on a daily basis before going home at night

♦ Post your goals in visible places as a constant reminder of their importance

♦ Focus on tying up all loose ends before closing out or submitting a project

Administration/Operational Support Goals

♦ Keep operational and administrative goals small and incremental so that they are readily achievable

♦ Regularly employ to-do lists and checklists to ensure that no step was skipped or overlooked

♦ Recognize personal productivity as a key career development tool

♦ Remain calm and focused when juggling multiple priorities to avoid appearing overwhelmed or stressed out

♦ Regularly communicate your questions or concerns to avoid unnecessary or unproductive activities

♦ Take interruptions in stride so as not to break your focus or lose sight of your end goal

Individual Contributor Goals

♦ Regularly set goals using your daily planner at the start of your day

♦ Set concrete, realistic goals that are readily achievable by a specific date

♦ Establish performance goals, not outcome goals, over which you can have maximum control

♦ Base your goals on personal performance so that you can keep control over their achievement

♦ Set precise goals, including completion dates, times, and specific outcomes, so that you can measure your progress

♦ Regularly modify your goals to reflect your changing priorities by scheduling incremental reviews in your electronic calendar

♦ Finish whatever you start out to do

Front-Line Supervisory and Managerial Goals

♦ Employ goals that are SMART (specific, measurable, attainable, relevant, and time-bound)

♦ Help your team members distinguish between urgent goals (that demand immediate attention) and important goals (that lead to their own personal goal achievement)

♦ Coach your employees to focus on being both effective and efficient

♦ Focus your team on identifying the low-hanging fruit that will increase your organizational effectiveness and help us redirect the workflow in light of your department's changing needs

♦ Recognize that goals requiring you to raise the bar bring the greatest personal satisfaction

♦ Strengthen your team's organizational forecasting abilities to proactively address potential shortfalls

Senior Leader Goals

- ◆ Master reverse goal-setting techniques that allow you to start with your ultimate objective and then work backward to develop your plan

- ◆ Mentally prepare yourself for success by mapping out specific milestones that you need to reach, forecasting obstacles, and envisioning completion

- ◆ Set realistic but concrete deadlines for yourself to increase your sense of urgency

- ◆ Cost out your time and your staff's time to raise awareness of how much your team's time is really worth and to set priorities accordingly

- ◆ Focus on measurable outcomes, set incremental milestone targets, and celebrate your victories and successes

- ◆ No matter how busy you are or how many priorities you're juggling, leave time for fun

Work-Life Balance

Early Career Goals

♦ Maintain a conscious balance between your work life and personal life

♦ Balance at-work demands with off-work priorities and interests

♦ Make the appropriate work-life choices that allow for achievement, creativity, and fun both at work and at home

Administration/Operational Support Goals

♦ Always try to find a healthy work-life balance so that you never risk burning yourself out

♦ Leave personal issues at the door when you arrive each morning

♦ Remain conscious of work overload signs whenever you feel overwhelmed, overburdened, or stressed

♦ Don't allow dysfunctional workplace dynamics to weigh you down; keep things in perspective

♦ If you feel yourself becoming cynical, consider ways of improving your outlook

♦ Find creative alternatives to ease your workload

♦ Recognize that sometimes less is more and that lightening up can provide you with the enlightenment you need to enjoy yourself at work

Individual Contributor Goals

♦ Avoid any perception of insensitivity or impatience with others

- Avoid putting yourself in the perfectionist predicament
- Combat work overload by learning to say no where appropriate
- Build creative playtime into your daily schedule
- Find the necessary balance to lead a healthful lifestyle
- Set healthy boundaries, and employ lots of white space to give yourself room to think
- Avoid accommodating others' needs out of guilt or a false sense of obligation

Front-Line Supervisory and Managerial Goals

- Ensure that the personal as well as professional needs of your direct reports are met
- Understand that individuals' personal problems may very well impact their work and employ the services of your EAP as a confidential resource to aid your team members
- Slow things down when work feels frenzied or out of control, and give your team members a chance to catch their breath and refocus
- Learn three nonwork things about each member of your team in order to build a stronger bond with them
- Use an 80–20 rule of thumb to separate work from personal issues
- Strive to focus primarily on work-related matters when dealing with your team members
- Publicly recognize employees who demonstrate work-life balance, and encourage staff members to focus on output rather than on hours for hours' sake

Senior Leader Goals

- Understand that beingness trumps doingness; don't always rush to accomplish *things*; instead, focus on the leader you want to be for others
- Focus on developing a caring-leadership culture based on character, integrity, and selflessness
- Recognize that, when your work life and personal life are out of balance, your stress level is likely to skyrocket

- Foster a culture that respects individual, customer, and organizational needs

- Create a more supportive work environment by increasing employees' sense of control

- Devote more resources to improving people management practices within your organization and to creating a more caring, selfless culture

PART II

PERFORMANCE APPRAISAL GOALS FOR PARTICULAR TITLES AND ROLES

Accounting and Finance

Accountant

- Complete monthly and quarterly reports on time and error free
- Always gain necessary signature approvals for budget variances
- Record all journal entries, account reconciliations, and monthly closing procedures accurately and in a timely fashion
- Code and enter invoices into our accounts payable system within 72 hours of arrival
- Thoroughly flag and reconcile financial discrepancies and variances
- Accurately prepare general ledger reconciliations of balance sheet accounts
- Proactively lead all month-end close activities to include journal entries, journal postings, account reconciliation, and general ledger analysis
- Become more confident in answering accounting procedural questions with authority
- Maintain flawless cash management schedules and bank reconciliations
- Be careful not to show resistance when asked to customize ad hoc financial reports
- Consistently complete database backups at appropriate intervals
- Organize AP checks from weekly check runs for vendor distribution using the appropriate mail drop codes
- Proactively develop and implement process and system improvements
- Prepare cost forecasts by evaluating and projecting cost data, updating cost estimates, and presenting revised pricing recommendations
- Willingly assist in the budgeting and forecasting process when opportunities arise

- Work more closely with the controller on the month-end closing process
- Assume lead responsibilities when interacting with internal auditors during our quarterly and annual audits
- Prepare deposits and accounting entries daily for miscellaneous cash receipts
- Always look to interpret the significance behind the numbers
- Demonstrate a broader mastery of generally accepted accounting principles
- Aggressively monitor expenditures by identifying variances and implementing corrective actions
- Regularly prepare a postaudit analysis for all capital and operational budget projects
- Act as the primary liaison between corporate accounting and each of your business units, providing general accounting assistance as needed
- Hold yourself fully accountable for the integrity of the database content
- Regularly ensure that reporting time lines are followed and managed effectively
- Readily assist in developing and implementing policies and procedures that sync up with all compliance audit standards and SOX (Sarbanes-Oxley) compliance requirements
- Maintain and balance subsidiary accounts more accurately by verifying, allocating, posting, and reconciling transactions

Auditor

- Participate more actively in audit planning discussions
- Strengthen your approach to audit planning by reviewing the annual operational plan objectives relating to the audit scope up front and identifying potential risks
- Create a risk/control matrix template for each key business process
- Discuss the assessment of basic controls (ABCs) with your team in advance of an audit launch
- Flag any relevant risks identified in our divisional risk map or risk/control matrix
- Proactively flag deficiencies in controls, fraud, or lack of compliance with laws, government regulations, or company policies and procedures

- Do a more thorough job of assessing risks and documenting controls
- Clearly distinguish between manual and automated controls
- Identify control and efficiency opportunities in the audit execution stage
- Calibrate your preliminary findings at the end of the first week with the rest of the team to verify that the scope of work and time lines are appropriate
- Keep assessing the design and operating effectiveness of controls throughout the audit
- Discuss processes and risk assessments with other staff members more frequently, keeping them apprised of any potential red flags
- Clearly document the results of your testing activities
- Issue findings or suggestions for business process improvements only after agreeing on an action plan with the relevant functional owner
- Minimize postaudit confusion by committing your findings, action plans, and proposed completion dates to paper
- Present your audit findings and business process improvement recommendations in a compelling manner during the close meeting
- Share best practices more regularly with your team members
- Willingly assist on other audit sections where work may be completed early
- Participate in different audit projects to gain a broader understanding of company applications, systems, and business processes
- Develop innovative, actionable, and cost-effective solutions to mitigate risk exposure and improve operating efficiencies
- When reporting your audit results, always include the outcome of your assessment of the risk environment as well as the recommended controls
- Provide more proactive leadership and mentoring to the internal audit staff to achieve audit goals and objectives
- Strengthen your ability to multitask by working on multiple audits in different phases

Bookkeeper

- Maintain subsidiary accounts more accurately by verifying transactions prior to posting

- Comply with federal, state, and local legal requirements by advising management on needed actions and by being willing to say no
- Display a higher level of customer service when dealing with creditors
- Prepare more compelling financial reports by analyzing account information and summarizing trends
- Balance subsidiary accounts by reconciling entries on a timely basis
- Process expense reports monthly, and flag any projected travel expense balances that may exceed budget
- Resolve account and billing issues more aggressively and consistently without having to be asked
- Build your skills and knowledge in the area of full-cycle accounting and generally accepted accounting procedures
- Increase your attentiveness to detail, and demonstrate a high level of accuracy
- Report research results that are thorough, relevant, and up-to-date
- Develop a reliable system to account for financial transactions by establishing a chart of accounts and defining bookkeeping policies and procedures
- Immediately escalate complex transactions that require additional approvals
- Independently gather and process financial information from contracted providers
- Provide hands-on assistance with general ledger entries as well as A/P, A/R, and daily cash entries
- Do a more thorough job with account analysis and reconciliations that are required for creating monthly financial statements
- Focus on strengthening your multitasking skills for the high-volume atmosphere you work in
- Avoid appearing to neglect sorting the mail, distributing it, and other administrative parts of your job
- Develop your level of expertise when dealing with financial software as well as QuickBooks, Excel, Word, and Outlook
- Balance the general ledger more efficiently by transferring subsidiary account summaries, preparing a trial balance, and reconciling entries
- Contribute to team and departmental goodwill by sharing your knowledge more willingly, giving financial guidance as appropriate, and creating a more inclusive work environment

♦ Hold yourself fully accountable for all levels of accounts payable coding, posting, and processing

Controller

♦ Create dashboard metrics that reflect financial, capital, and manpower planning needs

♦ Hold your team accountable for all aspects of preparation review and analysis of financial statements, general ledger, budgets, and year-end reviews

♦ Aggressively manage cash flow and credit to meet our operational needs

♦ Direct all essential accounting operational functions in an efficient and accurate manner

♦ Help set organizational policies and procedures by educating your nonfinancial peers about compliance and budget guidelines

♦ Participate more actively in the development of sales and financial reporting systems

♦ Regularly ensure the accuracy and timeliness of data entry for accounting transactions, source documents, and records

♦ Identify and develop methods geared toward providing management with information vital to the decision-making process

♦ Take ownership of the global accounting close to minimize closing time and to ensure that closing tasks are performed in a timely and accurate fashion

♦ Look for periodic opportunities and find new ways of disseminating financial information to corporate management

♦ Understand that your role encompasses involvement in a broad range of accounting *and administrative* activities essential to the maintenance of day-to-day operations

♦ Create and maintain an accurate record of all company assets and liabilities to appropriately reflect the company's financial condition

♦ Proactively manage any accounting system software upgrades and conversions

♦ Participate more actively in our strategic planning efforts, highlighting the corporate financial perspective of intended actions

♦ Provide greater oversight to the accounting department in its relationships with auditors, bankers, and related vendors

♦ Always model expected organizational behaviors for your team

- Regularly suggest ways to improve profitability
- Establish more robust internal controls to improve the flow and reliability of information
- Closely oversee the daily, monthly, and year-end financial closing processes
- Proactively identify and coordinate all capital investment needs
- Provide more guidance and structure in budgeting and forecasting
- Consistently ensure that all supporting transactions are completed and posted in a timely manner
- Regularly monitor and communicate product utilization trends to support pricing strategies
- Aggressively manage the collection of accounts receivable to generate cash flow
- Manage your workflow throughout the year more efficiently in anticipation of the year-end audit requirements
- Support divisional management with reporting operational information according to the proper accounting methodology
- Build financial and operational decision-making models using sophisticated trend analysis and forecasting techniques
- Ensure that parent-level results are in compliance with corporate and GAAP reporting requirements
- Ensure that all reported financial results are clearly understood and comprehensively explained
- Work more closely with the financial planning and analysis team to identify inefficiencies, redundancies, and duplicative efforts
- Develop a more reliable cash flow projection process and reporting mechanism to meet operating needs
- Optimize the handling of banking relationships. and initiate appropriate strategies to enhance cash positions
- Strengthen your database software skills to better quantify and illustrate complex financial reports, comparisons, and projections
- Coordinate the timely preparation of monthly, quarterly, and annual consolidated financial statements on a cash and GAAP basis
- Assume responsibility for the tax function, including federal, multistate, and local income, sales, business, property, and withholding tax return planning and compliance
- Evaluate recurring monthly procedures looking for opportunities for process and control improvements

- Identify areas for automation and maximum utilization of new accounting system software
- Serve as the primary technical sounding board for the CFO when the complex interpretation of GAAP is required
- Develop and monitor greater controls that safeguard company assets
- Strictly monitor all Sarbanes-Oxley and internal control compliance in accordance with appropriate GAAP standards

Credit and Collections Manager

- Regularly interact with customers to ensure that their credit lines remain open
- Establish team targets and associated metrics to evaluate performance and shortfalls
- Manage all aspects of credit, accounts receivable, and collections with the primary goal of maximizing cash flow while minimizing bad debt losses
- Review credit applications, customer financial statements, and credit reports more thoroughly when determining the creditworthiness of new customers
- Monitor and report on our collection agencies' results on a timely basis
- Assist your team members more readily in the collection of problem accounts
- Work more closely with our sales reps to establish credit for new customers and to resolve credit issues
- Flag problem accounts and suggest appropriate action plans
- Review accounts receivable aging reports on an ongoing basis and identify problem accounts with suggested solutions
- Prepare accurate and timely accounts receivable status reports
- Distribute reports to management at least on a monthly basis, but more often if circumstances require
- Regularly review all contracts in preparation of upcoming sales negotiations
- Set up regular weekly staff meetings with the accounts receivable and credit teams to ensure open communication and to discuss departmental challenges

♦ Create a training checklist for new hires that includes UCC-1 filings, collections, check requests, customer debits and credits, and write-offs

♦ Monitor receivable aging reports and assist in account reconciliations and disputes

♦ Identify and flag uncollectible accounts on a timely basis

♦ Review and approve nonstandard terms and conditions according to strict company guidelines

♦ Develop a stronger understanding of letters of credit and guarantees as well as other instruments for mitigating risk

♦ Actively review letters of credit requirements and the discounting process

♦ Identify new and creative ways of assessing risk, whether through the formal review of contracts and financial statements or informal customer interviews

♦ Coordinate and align your department's efforts in interfacing with business segments, centers of excellence, and outsource providers

♦ Fine-tune your collection performance, risk assessment, and reserve process reporting

Financial Analyst

♦ Proactively identify and account for any budget variances

♦ Focus on broadening your overall financial reporting and analysis capabilities to include FTE reporting, revenue, reimbursements, financial planning, variable/contingency labor, and federal and state reporting

♦ Monitor overhead expenses more aggressively via effective cost analysis

♦ Play a more significant role in the annual budget process by providing training, access, and budget preparation guidance to line management

♦ Proactively develop and implement process and system improvements

♦ Review comparative year-over-year data to spot trends and patterns, draw conclusions, and frame options for further consideration

♦ Continuously monitor the external operating, competitor, and regulatory environments

- Hold yourself fully accountable for the integrity of the database content
- Regularly ensure that reporting time lines are followed and managed effectively
- Always demonstrate a proactive and solution-oriented approach toward business problems and process improvements
- Demonstrate a keen eye for detail when projecting future expenditures
- Strengthen your ability to build rapport, cultivate working relationships, and drive collaboration across business teams
- Expand your skills and responsibilities to include customer penetration as well as revenue and renewal rate analysis
- Resolve data issues in a timely manner to mitigate downtime and ensure data integrity
- Suggest adjustments to the current suite of management reports in order to reflect changes in your operating environment
- Vigorously flag any accounting regularities or potential conflicts of interest
- Strengthen your business-planning and acquisitions-modeling skills
- Create human capital metrics that highlight the return-on-investment of the company's salary and benefits expenditures
- Demonstrate a stronger understanding of accounting, including the interrelations among the balance sheet, income, and cash flow statements
- Increase your efficiency in utilizing self-service tools to extract data for analysis
- Readily assist in developing and implementing policies and procedures that sync up with all compliance audit standards and SOX (Sarbanes-Oxley) compliance requirements
- Be better prepared to facilitate audits performed by corporate or external regulatory agencies

Human Resources

Benefits Administrator

- Field calls from employees with a positive sense of customer service regarding health, dental, life, disability, leaves of absence, 401(k) administration, and PTO
- Assist in the analysis, design, delivery, and administration of all benefit programs for active, former, and retired employees
- Ensure that all benefits plans are in compliance with applicable statutes and regulations
- Maintain all benefits files in compliance with established record retention requirements
- Provide the initial response to employee benefit questions, and escalate to another resource within 24 hours if you can't resolve the matter at your level
- Serve as your company's primary contact with benefits vendors for resolution of employee issues regarding workers' comp, FMLA, and short- and long-term disability
- Work closely with your company's benefits consulting firm to ensure that employees' questions are handled as they relate to claims, enrollment, and eligibility
- Immediately escalate any significant benefit challenges for directors and above
- Remain aware of the precedent-setting nature of your department's decisions
- Present the benefits portion of employee orientation, and assist new hires with benefits enrollment
- Accurately calculate premiums for life insurance self-billing arrangements

- Publicize and draw attention to some of the lesser known benefits offered to ensure that the company gets the greatest return on investment for its benefit dollars

- Reconcile invoices for payment on a biweekly basis

- Immediately flag benefit statement variances for your supervisor's review

- Assume primary responsibility for bringing billing reconciliation and invoice breakdowns to the finance department's attention

- Regularly review all HR department invoices for accuracy and prepare them for submission to accounts payable

- Ensure the timely distribution of all plan-level communications, including summary plan descriptions (SPDs) and summary annual reports (SARs)

- Accurately enter and maintain all benefits-related information in the HRIS system

- Volunteer to support the HRIS administrator whenever your workload slows down

- Ensure that employees are educated on the company's various benefits programs via new hire orientation, open enrollment, and our health and wellness fairs

- Partner with the payroll department to process any payroll deductions that must sync with the payroll cycle

- Willingly assist with the administration of various compensation-related projects as necessary, including the corporate bonus and restricted stock unit programs

- Review market data and published benchmarking surveys in order to recommend program updates and new offerings

- Keep abreast of trends and best practices in benefits design

- Enroll in a workshop on the so-called devil's triangle of FMLA, workers' comp, and the Americans with Disabilities Act

- Properly coordinate leaves of absence and returns to work in accordance with an employee's medical certification

- Allow current employees' positions to be backfilled only after gaining appropriate legal approval from outside counsel

- Insist that employees' medical certifications contain information regarding both the frequency and duration of their leaves

- Ensure that medical records are kept separate from other personnel records

◆ Retain all e-mails relating to an employee's leave of absence in a separate e-mail folder organized by the employee's name and date(s) of leave(s)

◆ Steadfastly comply with ERISA's reporting and disclosure requirements

◆ Maintain procedural documentation to reflect any changes in interpretation to your company's benefits policies or practices

◆ Understand that COBRA requires that coverage be identical to similarly situated active plan participants in terms of (1) benefits, (2) deductibles, and (3) coverage limits

◆ Ensure compliance with benefits-related regulations and changing legislation relating to COBRA, HIPAA, FMLA, and ERISA

◆ Actively promote the benefits of participating in your company's 401(k) plan

Compensation Analyst

◆ Review and update both the compensation and noncompensation dimensions of the company's total rewards system

◆ Develop internal career paths, leveling, and titling as the company rolls out the new technical progression plan in the new year

◆ Document compensation plan decisions to ensure compliance with government regulations

◆ Act as an internal consultant to our organization on compensation issues, incorporating both industry best practices and competitive benchmarks

◆ Procure new market intelligence by regularly participating in market surveys

◆ Avoid e-mailing other organizations directly for compensation data to avoid any perception of colluding on the price of labor

◆ Strengthen your knowledge of employment and pay discrimination issues, especially regarding the Equal Pay Act

◆ Flag potential variances when comparing proposed pay increases with budget

◆ Collaborate with clients to evaluate job duties and to determine appropriate market pricing

◆ Regularly evaluate new positions for external competitiveness and internal equity

- Ensure that new hire salaries are anywhere within a range of plus or minus 15% of the statistical average

- Support the recruitment team with internal transfer and promotion requests by explaining how internal equity data and salary range caps affect their salary requests

- Immediately research any compensation concerns raised by recruiters during the recruitment process

- Serve as the subject matter expert to hiring managers on pay decisions and other compensation-related matters

- Follow all eligibility guidelines closely before assuming that an employee is entitled to participate in a particular bonus plan

- Work closely with finance when administering our variable compensation programs, especially corporate bonuses, stock options, and restricted stock units (RSUs)

- Explain to supervisors the necessary considerations in awarding promotions

- Conduct ongoing job analysis and evaluation activities to ensure the proper classification of jobs

- Don't hesitate to evaluate and recommend upgrades to the performance appraisal and merit pay programs

- Analyze and recommend process and system improvements to support the compensation function

- Familiarize yourself with the design of variable compensation programs, especially in light of the company's upcoming profit-sharing plan and sales incentive program

- Always verify that operating and capital budgets can support any exceptions that you propose before escalating your recommendation to corporate

- Review salary increases for compliance with the organization's policy and budget

- Analyze key compensation reporting metrics to identify trends or patterns of statistical significance

- Assist in creating a high-performance culture where the commission structure incentivizes the right behaviors to drive sales

- Actively provide guidance on the administration of pay programs by explaining your rationale for denying requests for large salary increases that exceed company pay practices

- Compile and report financial data for the board's compensation committee, knowing that your recommendations will be highly scrutinized

- Obtain the appropriate authorizations from finance before approving any additions to head count or promotional increases in excess of 10%
- Rely on existing salary ranges and competitive market data to justify any exceptions to the pay recommendations you make
- Quantify any potential variance and wait to receive e-mail approval from finance before communicating with clients
- Participate on design teams with business partners from the business unit, HR, and finance to design incentive plans that support the business strategy
- Conduct market competitiveness reviews, benchmarking/best practice studies, and other analytical research to ensure that your compensation structure remains both competitive and reasonable
- Conduct in-depth market pricing analysis by comparing like organizations by size, industry, geography, and function
- Look to reporting relationships, span of control, and size of budget when comparing individual roles and job classifications to the external market
- Remain cognizant of significant business changes and their potential impact on compensation practices, including acquisitions or divestitures, changes in accounting or tax practices, and extraordinary P&L items
- Work independently to resolve more complex employee and management inquiries related to compensation policies and practices
- Serve as the lead resource in developing and administering compensation and salary programs that consider both internal and external equity
- Regularly analyze positions, hourly wages, salaries, and incentives to evaluate internal equity, external competitiveness, and legal compliance of our organization's pay practices
- Look for creative ways to justify potential exceptions to the pay grade structure

Employee and Labor Relations Representative

- Develop human capital ROI metrics to quantify the impact of workforce investments
- Identify the human capital drivers of organizational success

- Project future trends in employee performance on a monthly, quarterly, and annual basis

- Share trends in voluntary turnover with front-line supervisors so that they can manage employee relations more effectively

- Strengthen the muscle of your client management team by proactively educating them on so-called third-rail topics that are not subject to corrective action and that may result in immediate termination

- Ensure the consistent application of workplace rules and policies to ensure fairness and avoid claims of discrimination

- Consistently manage out substandard job performers via documented corrective action and construct defensible terminations for cause

- Conduct appropriate layoff analysis in cases of projected reductions in force

- Effectively mediate disputes in your client groups, and address problem situations head-on

- Strengthen your progressive disciplinary writing skills when addressing issues that typically fall under the radar but that must be brought to the employees' attention nevertheless

- Continue to focus on the legal aspects of employee relations to strengthen your gut response and self-confidence when asked for initial recommendations by your clients

- Consistently involve the compensation team in any matters that potentially impact pay or payroll practices

- Provide wise advice and counsel to management and employees alike

- Always share up front that you may have an obligation to disclose potential conflicts of interest with the company and cannot guarantee confidentiality

- Partner with division and department managers to help them lead more effectively

- Serve as a front-line resource to both managers and employees who look to HR as a resource for confidential career advice and organizational best practices

- Ensure consistency, transparency, and full disclosure in all matters relating to Sarbanes-Oxley (SOX) compliance

- Engage in routine, one-on-one employee discussions in an effort to sustain two-way, free-flowing communication between management and staff level personnel

- Provide direction and interpretive feedback to all personnel with regard to the company's annual employee opinion survey
- Devise action plans and feedback sessions to maximize the value of the exit interview program
- Effectively advise the leadership team on identifying and adapting measurable goals regarding employee satisfaction
- Lead and conduct employee investigations with an eye toward reaching a sound conclusion in a reasonable time frame
- Ensure that steps of progressive discipline are not skipped in the areas of substandard job performance or attendance
- Readily escalate cases of egregious misconduct to either termination or a final written warning—even for a first offense
- Ensure that the corrective action response fits the transgression, and avoid overdisciplining for *de minimis* infractions
- Ensure legal compliance for all leaves of absence, including FMLA, ADA, and worker's compensation matters
- Aggressively challenge unwarranted unemployment claims and appeals
- Consider opportunities where the company may not want to contest unemployment in an effort to encourage an employee to voluntarily resign
- Regularly communicate changes in company personnel policies and procedures to ensure compliance
- Conduct employee meetings and walk-around sessions establishing effective continuity between HR and the workforce

Recruiter (Corporate)

- Actively source, screen, and schedule candidates for employment openings
- Confer with hiring managers before launching a search to identify job specifications, primary versus secondary duties, and candidate qualifications
- Identify new and refreshing ways to attract, retain, and develop top talent
- Creatively source hard-to-fill positions using social media, Internet data-mining techniques, professional networks, and internal referrals

- Build a network of senior-level candidates to strengthen our bench of talent

- Proactively qualify and profile plant managers, production supervisors, and warehouse managers where you have the highest turnover

- Focus on gaining a stronger understanding of all corporate positions you'll be recruiting for, including operations, finance, and IT

- Keep a critical eye on cost-per-hire metrics, and reduce your reliance on search firms

- Strengthen your direct sourcing capabilities in the areas of manufacturing and distribution

- Encourage passive job candidates to apply online even if they're not currently looking to change jobs at the time of your call

- Define your company's diversity outreach recruitment strategy more clearly

- Establish and maintain contacts with schools, alumni groups, and other public organizations to proactively build our applicant pool

- Coach and counsel managers through the hiring process to ensure optimal hiring within an acceptable timeframe

- Build and develop your social media recruitment outreach strategy to include LinkedIn, Facebook, and Twitter in addition to online job boards

- Employ behavior-based interviewing questions to ensure spontaneous and unrehearsed answers from candidates

- Invite hiring managers to partner with you during reference-checking calls so that they can hear directly from prior supervisors how to best manage a candidate

- Customize your reference checks to match a candidate's personality to your company's corporate culture

- Consistently track and document status and communication with all applicants in your applicant tracking system (ATS)

- Extend employment offers only after reference and background checks are complete

- Make all employment offers contingent on successfully passing drug screens and employee physicals

- Never extend an offer without a last-minute check of budget and head-count approvals

- Measure the recruitment program's success by establishing metrics like cost-per-hire, time-to-start, probationary turnover, and source cost analysis

- Demonstrate mastery of all federal and state employment laws, including all applicable EEO and ADA regulations
- Effectively manage our organization's EEO-1 and affirmative action programs to meet and exceed reporting standards
- Define areas of minority and female underutilization relative to our local employment community
- Outsource our temp desk with a goal of a 20% reduction in agency overhead fees
- Negotiate contingency search firm fees down from 33% to 25%
- Maintain contact with candidates through their two-week notice period to ensure that they don't suffer from buyer's remorse and fall prey to counteroffers at their current companies
- Measure internal promotions as a percentage of filled jobs
- Budget an internal finders' fee program that is one-tenth the cost of the typical cost-per-hire
- Follow up with new hires after one week and then 30 days later to ensure a smooth transition into the company
- Establish an effective onboarding program to lower probationary turnover

Training and Organizational Development Specialist

- Design effective training materials and programs for the corporate classroom, including web-based and e-learning environments
- Demonstrate a thorough understanding of adult learning theory that appeals to diverse learning styles
- Work closely with operational management to conduct needs assessments and deliver programs on a problem-to-solution level
- Create a template for data collection, data analysis, and managerial reporting to enable apples-to-apples comparisons of training roll-outs and program effectiveness
- Facilitate the logistics for all upcoming programs and workshops
- Effectively manage all aspects of our learning management system (LMS), and interface with the application vendor for system maintenance and support
- Collaborate regularly with the HR generalist team to assess each department's learning needs

- Regularly communicate training courses and schedules in consultation with departmental decision makers via newsletters, e-mail, and the company intranet

- Develop stronger personal relationships with subject matter experts to create a greater sense of teamwork and camaraderie

- Create interactive multimedia training applications that make use of the full functionality of our system's capabilities

- Constantly monitor organizational training goals and objectives to develop training materials that address any skills gaps

- Develop a broad curriculum of offerings, including technical and soft skills workshops as well as compliance modules

- Regularly assess and recommend off-the-shelf courseware packages to complement internal training offerings

- Routinely follow up with trainees to ensure practical concept application

- Create metrics on end user progress that demonstrate the effectiveness of learning and development programs

- Proactively recommend training improvement strategies based on participant feedback

- Develop and deploy a training feedback survey that pinpoints areas for improvement in delivery as well as content

- Use your creativity and imagination to create dynamic, interactive, and fun educational experiences to optimize learning

- Recognize that people learn more from stories that they can relate to than from policies and rules; customize your content to make your material more memorable

- Focus on developing stronger organizational/industry knowledge to strengthen your credibility with the group

- Enroll in a public speaking course to increase the *gravitas* necessary to command the room's attention

- When planning course offerings, consider all aspects of implementation, including rollout logistics, budget and resource allocation, and necessary corporate approvals

- Hold yourself accountable for projecting strategic workforce planning needs

- Boost your evaluation scores by injecting more humor and levity into your presentations

- Effectively address trainee performance or conduct problems, and share your findings with trainees' immediate supervisors

- Regularly evaluate your progress and measure the effectiveness of your courses to determine whether program objectives are being met

- Maintain an active network of industry trainers and executive coaches

- Adhere to standard formats for all content, ensuring consistent quality for all deliverables

- Employ a curriculum development methodology that is consistent with American Society for Training and Development (ASTD) best practices in assessment, design, development, measurement, and evaluation

- Tie all content whenever possible to your company's mission, vision, and values

- Engage your audience more by making your presentations more interactive and by encouraging greater participation in discussions

- Strengthen your platform skills by taping your presentations and concentrating on your body language and hand gesture usage

Information Technology

Database Administrator

- Proactively monitor the database systems to ensure minimum downtime
- Clearly communicate requirements and resolution following downtime to both technical and nontechnical team members
- Ensure system stability and accessibility by monitoring performance and making recommendations for upgrades and enhancements
- Regularly oversee database backups, restores, and disaster recovery plans
- Consistently ensure a high level of system security
- Regularly assist programming teams with the development of databases, triggers, stored procedures, and other development-related tasks
- Modify database programs to increase processing performance (performance tuning)
- Develop and maintain the database administration guide used by programmers
- Assume total responsibility for ensuring system availability, usability, and survivability
- Independently maintain weekly data warehouse release processes
- Establish physical database initialization parameters for effective performance tuning
- Monitor and optimize system performance using index tuning and disk optimization
- Confer with coworkers to determine the impact of database changes on other systems

- Develop policies and procedures regarding security, backup schedules, restoration, and general development
- Regularly monitor and maintain appropriate disk storage requirements (capacity planning)
- Calculate the optimum values for database parameters, especially memory, to be used for each project
- Improve your delivery time in writing and tuning SQL scripts for data retrieval and reporting
- Provide on-call support and participate more actively in the on-call roster
- Strengthen your knowledge of development cycles and standards as well as server platforms
- Regularly review discrepant vendor invoices for database-related purchases and determine causes of errors
- Demonstrate greater adaptability to changing priorities and flexible workloads
- Do a more thorough job in handling general problems on your own authority, working more independently, and making sound judgments based on current information
- Assist users, peers, and management in the development of business cases for new systems or extensive system modifications
- Strengthen your knowledge of storage architecture developments as they relate to physical database design
- Ensure that your team assumes full responsibility for database architecture and maintenance

Help Desk Coordinator

- Regularly contribute to and support the operational stability of the desktop, network, and server environments
- Perform ongoing installation, repair, and preventive maintenance of PCs and related software/hardware
- Participate in a supportive role by providing telephone and in-person technical support
- Ensure that customer goals and service levels are met by responding to complex customer inquiries related to core software applications

- Provide leadership and work guidance to less experienced associates
- Respond to open tickets and accurately triage, and escalate work requests to second-level support when necessary
- Consistently communicate and follow up with customers to ensure that inquiries are resolved within the agreed-upon timeframes
- Demonstrate a greater willingness to perform shift work and overtime as well as weekend flexibility
- Readily resolve first-tier problems according to established service level agreements
- Immediately escalate complex problems to second- or third-tier support
- Become more adept at troubleshooting software and hardware failures and at identifying appropriate solutions for personal desktop computers
- Immediately record any exceptions to procedural guidelines
- Aggressively reduce help desk call rates by evaluating inquiry reports and making the necessary recommendations to prevent recurring problems
- Look for opportunities to assist project managers and participate in larger-scale projects
- Regularly recommend changes to policies and procedures to streamline operations
- Consistently log and track inquiries in the database, and maintain history records and related problem documentation
- Recognize, research, isolate, and recommend resolution procedures more confidently
- Prioritize customer problems and complaints, and clearly communicate expected time lines for resolution
- Compose help desk tickets that clearly specify the direction and steps necessary to support swift resolution of client challenges
- Strengthen your knowledge of Windows 7, Office 2010, and networking fundamentals
- Obtain entry-level IT Infrastructure Library (ITIL) global service desk certification in the upcoming year
- Demonstrate a stronger understanding of requisite help desk tools, processes, and methodologies
- Conduct proactive data mining to identify the top five trouble ticket items and reduce incoming call volume

Programmer Analyst

♦ Regularly perform the analysis, systems design, coding, documentation, testing, and implementation of all business applications

♦ Proactively test, maintain, and monitor computer programs and systems

♦ Analyze user requirements, procedures, and problems to improve existing computer systems

♦ Implement and design systems in accordance with company methodology

♦ Maintain audit trails, conduct periodic reviews, and ensure audit records are archived for future reference

♦ Understand the relationship between key data stores and application programs

♦ Demonstrate a greater understanding of the company's systems architectures, including how these systems fit within the overall business

♦ Effectively communicate project status updates with clients and peers

♦ Participate in the development and documentation of backup plans for all existing server applications

♦ Regularly consult with customers about their software system and technical design needs

♦ Analyze complex system needs and problems more thoroughly

♦ Execute production and programming fixes in support of critical system functions

♦ Demonstrate expert-level knowledge with implementing, maintaining, scaling, tuning, and deploying SQL server solutions

♦ Develop system design solutions that consistently exceed client expectations

♦ Design, develop, and modify software systems using object-oriented programming languages and appropriate client server applications as well as development processes

♦ Be more willing to adjust your schedule to accommodate off-hour systems

♦ Formulate and document specifications for computer programmers to use in coding, testing, and debugging computer programs

♦ Prepare milestone status reports and deliverables for end-user representatives

- Monitor information system performance and system recovery processes to ensure that security features and procedures are properly restored
- Stay current on technical issues that influence supported technologies
- Learn and adapt new technology to business and technical problems
- Attend technical conferences and seminars to develop your knowledge of full life cycle development: new development, system enhancements, testing, and implementation
- Strengthen your team's knowledge of current storage and retrieval methods
- Serve as a mentor to junior programming staff and as a knowledge resource for other programmers on where to source data, how it is used, and how and when it is created
- Develop specialized knowledge in at least one core programming language

Project Manager

- Invest more time up front to gain a clearer understanding of the deliverables required for upcoming programs
- Regularly monitor significant issue tracking and ongoing cost analyses
- Manage budgets more effectively by monitoring project status in comparison to cost/time projections
- Provide more consistent and comprehensive status reports and project updates
- Ensure that implementation standards are established that best suit the client's business requirements and that adhere to budget and time line constraints
- Develop stronger communication strategies and approaches for service implementation
- Ensure alignment across organizations to meet or exceed the customer target date
- Foster relationships with clients at both the project and executive sponsor levels
- Manage contracts more aggressively, ensuring that suppliers perform in accordance with original agreements
- Obtain your Project Management Professional certification through the Project Management Institute within the next 12–18 months

- Regularly track and trend on-time, on-budget, and quality metrics
- Deliver a total solution that meets requirements and that exceeds customer expectations
- Assume responsibility for the full scope of projects, including resource scheduling, project tracking, risk analysis, and cost management
- Do a more effective job of keeping longer-term projects on schedule
- Consistently follow defined quality control testing procedures to maintain the overall quality of deliverables
- Proactively communicate status, budget, and time line updates to the account team
- Adhere to project management methodology guidelines to manage the entire project life cycle
- Develop stronger team collaboration skills, including coaching, mentoring, and advising
- Thoroughly analyze and document the customer's business and technical requirements before recommending appropriate solutions
- Polish your presentation, demonstration, training, and facilitation abilities
- Strengthen your knowledge of industry-standard project methods, tools, and techniques

Systems Analyst

- Regularly enforce server and workstation configuration standards
- Focus on producing higher quality functional system documentation
- Develop and deliver a weekly trend analysis of system load, usage, and response
- Ensure that backup/recovery strategies are planned and implemented consistently
- Bridge the communication gap between development teams and business sponsors
- Regularly support the quality assurance team through the testing cycle, and provide oversight and assessment on system defects
- Explain and define system requirements in layman's terms without technical jargon

- Ensure that your team proactively maintains system security functions

- Supervise server upgrades and migration to new server-level software in accordance with scheduled time lines and commitments

- Investigate, debug, and solve customer questions and problems on a timely basis

- Work in concert with platform managers and hardware service technicians to proactively troubleshoot server failures and accessibility problems

- Regularly monitor system performance and track usage of enterprise management software

- Partner with the project manager, and assume a lead role in assessing project scope and feasibility

- Communicate more effectively with cross-functional departments to define requirements and objectives for new applications

- Participate more actively in architecture, technical design, and product implementation discussions

- Establish stronger relationships with commercial vendors to ensure smoother coordination of system support and upgrades

- Look for opportunities to perform low-level system engineering and integration functions

- Assume responsibility for the full life cycle of design, development, testing, implementation, and documentation of new applications

- Coordinate with server and workstation tech support to ensure that computer servers and workstations operate at optimal performance and capacity

- Provide user training and technical support in a more customer-friendly fashion

- Enroll in a certification program focusing on a higher-level programming language like Java, C++, or C#

- Demonstrate a stronger working knowledge of scripting languages

- Look for opportunities to gain greater exposure to browsers, cookies, and Web-focused analysis tools

Legal

Attorney

♦ Increase your rainmaking efforts by developing a higher volume of quality clients

♦ Develop preventive law and compliance programs to reduce the company exposure to legal risk

♦ Regularly ensure legal, fiscal, and operational protocol and compliance

♦ Conduct extensive and well-reasoned legal research to develop optimal strategies on behalf of our clients

♦ Analyze complex legal and factual issues with an eye toward opposing counsel's position

♦ Independently prepare complex pleadings, written discovery, depositions, motions, and briefs in support of your legal strategies

♦ Always hold yourself accountable for the prompt, efficient, and effective disposition of assigned cases

♦ Provide effective and timely advice and counsel to internal management as needed

♦ Communicate with the court, witnesses, and opposing counsel in a manner consistent with established civil procedure guidelines

♦ Provide effective and timely communication, information, and legal advice to clients on legal and factual issues

♦ Assume responsibility for orchestrating outside counsel activities in larger-scale projects

♦ Work more independently and effectively at preparing witnesses and evidence for trial

♦ Confidently advise clients on matters related to corporate transactions and regulatory compliance

- Demonstrate greater flexibility in collaborating with other in-house attorneys
- Build and develop more effective relationships with your clients
- Focus on winning the respect, trust, and confidence of your peers as both a subject matter expert and a senior leader on your team
- Strategically anticipate the legal risks of pending business deals
- Continue to hone your jury presentation skills by making compelling arguments in a more comfortable and relaxed manner
- Avoid any appearance of condescending behavior when dealing with nonattorney peers
- Provide timely responses to federal, state, and local regulatory inquiries
- Comply at all times with the code of professional responsibility governing lawyerly conduct
- Pursue opportunities to expand your firm's brand visibility in the community
- Develop your litigation and appeals practice to include mediation and private case management
- Develop your team's abilities to render legal opinions and to formulate conclusions that will withstand regulatory scrutiny
- Search for ways to maximize the efficiency and utilization of your attorney/paralegal teams
- Actively counsel department leaders regarding policy changes, best practice guidelines, and optimal courses of action
- Determine whether matters should be litigated offensively or defensively or whether settlement efforts should be made
- Look for opportunities to become more involved in structuring and negotiating strategic dispute resolutions and settlements
- Select outside legal counsel in terms of both legal expertise and cost containment
- Monitor and flag trends and changes in the law as reflected in judicial precedent, legislation, and government regulations
- Become more adept at and confident in handling basic corporate legal issues without guidance
- Attend legal education seminars to generate sufficient continuing education credits

Contract Analyst

♦ Flag urgent contractual items that require immediate review

♦ Ensure the accuracy of contract documents for deal presentation

♦ Implement and update contract documents in response to policy or rule changes

♦ Engage in quality control– and compliance-related reviews of contract acceptances and executions

♦ Review and provide quality assurance oversight for contract expirations

♦ Regularly ensure timely notice of contract expirations

♦ Ensure that contract documents are archived appropriately and available for future reference

♦ Perform spot audits of random contracts to ensure that quality control standards are being met

♦ Create documentation checklists to identify potential problems and ensure consistent contract administration

♦ Ensure that incoming change orders, interim agreements, and amendments are tracked and catalogued appropriately

♦ Regularly archive and mail counterparty confirmations to ensure fulfillment requirements

♦ Demonstrate a greater understanding of the contract management database and contract administration continuum

♦ Look for new opportunities to lead projects focused on improving the contract operations process

♦ Pay closer attention to incorporating proposed amendments into contract revisions

♦ Offer recommendations for streamlining and improving the contract management process

♦ Consistently follow all standard operating procedures when processing contracts, keeping a special eye on Sarbanes-Oxley (SOX) guidelines and regulations

♦ Draft, negotiate, and execute vendor contracts in compliance with standard operating procedures

♦ Ensure that suppliers meet all compliance regulations before initiating a new contract

♦ Always secure the necessary internal approvals before drafting a contract offering

- Ensure that all contract recommendations are vetted and approved prior to distribution
- Analyze any change requests to existing contracts, and recommend changes or revisions as appropriate
- Create reports on the share drive that will show the approval status of pending contracts
- Generate compliant offers and corresponding contracts that meet both business and customer needs
- Develop a contract implementation strategy to explore alternatives and exceptions to past practices
- Identify and flag any discrepancies that fall outside contract guidelines
- Always add counterparty confirmations of receipt to the upper left-hand side of the contract folder
- Thoroughly document all exceptions and approvals in the contract management master log
- Identify and provide guidance to internal clients regarding contractual exceptions to standard business and pricing programs
- Review and revamp any shortcomings or glitches in the contract lifecycle process
- Customize any terms and conditions that fall outside the contract template structure
- Develop an approved exceptions list to ensure greater flexibility in amending template contracts for one-off situations
- Obtain the necessary approvals within agreed-upon time frames from the sales, finance, and legal departments
- Consistently track and save all previous versions of contractual templates

Legal Secretary

- Strictly observe standards of professional conduct and confidentiality at all times
- Meet all deadlines and filing requirements without exception
- Schedule and maintain calendars of appointments, meetings, and travel itineraries without breaking a sweat or appearing to be overwhelmed

- Demonstrate a stronger working knowledge of court structures and legal resources
- Be prepared to compose—not just type—legal documents with minimal instruction
- Consistently resolve workflow problems to maintain effective and efficient office operations
- Maintain clean and immaculate client files that can withstand internal audit challenges
- Communicate in advance any time you believe you may not be able to meet an upcoming filing deadline so that additional resources can be assigned to assist you
- Administer all pleadings in the proper discovery formats
- Stay ahead of supply and equipment needs so that the office runs smoothly and efficiently at all times
- Look for ways to increase efficiency so that you can support a larger caseload
- Effectively juggle the diverse responsibilities of assisting with client document execution, the billing process, time entry, and calendar maintenance
- Ensure the proper maintenance of all computer-based litigation support systems
- Learn to constructively and diplomatically balance your responsibilities when you're pulled in too many directions
- Strengthen your redline editing abilities by taking clearer notes and proofing your work
- Be careful not to appear to pick and choose the partners you work for or the assignments you take on
- Strengthen your legal writing skills by mastering the proper format for citations, footnotes, and cross-references
- Minimize interruption from outside phone calls by qualifying callers more thoroughly
- Clearly set nonclients' expectations in terms of ability to respond to their calls
- Track and report billable hour computations accurately and in a timely fashion
- Always apply the highest attention to detail, especially when working a 2:1 desk for a partner and an associate
- Look for ways to excel and multitask in our fast-paced, deadline-driven environment

- Enroll in an internal training course to strengthen your knowledge of state and federal court e-filing procedures
- Continue to create high-quality visuals for bound and indexed client presentations
- Successfully juggle the competing priorities of generating legal pleadings, discovery, and internal record preparation
- Strictly preserve privileged and confidential attorney-client information

Paralegal

- Identify and flag nonstandard contractual issues that may pose a risk to the company
- Investigate pending customer account issues before recommending contract renewals or terminations
- Track, maintain, and organize all legal files in an organized manner
- Vet contract issues with finance before submitting your final recommendations
- Increase your turnaround time in locating statutes and case law on the LexisNexis and Westlaw online database systems
- Regularly monitor licensees to ensure that they fulfill their contractual obligations
- Actively maintain the electronic legal research software and law library
- Ensure the proper updating of all computer-based litigation support systems
- Proactively research codes and regulations at issue in contract negotiations
- Diligently respond to client issues that arise after contract execution
- Demonstrate greater efficiency when gathering, analyzing, and organizing documents pertaining to pretrial litigation
- Skillfully prepare draft pleadings and discovery documents for trial attorneys' review
- Show greater attention to detail when assembling, proofing, and editing drafts of contracts and licenses
- Double-check your work when preparing first-draft contracts for use with customers

- Look for opportunities to provide administrative support to the legal department whenever possible
- Accurately draft standardized contracts using template documents
- Prepare contract modifications, amendments, and revisions in strict compliance with partner directives
- Demonstrate a stronger understanding of civil litigation terminology
- Know your contracts better, in terms of both approval status and upcoming deadlines
- Review powers of attorney and trust documents before the client's arrival to ensure a smooth and successful transaction
- Prepare and file proofs of claim and fee applications on a timely basis
- Strictly observe standards of professional conduct and confidentiality at all times

Manufacturing

Assembly and Packaging Technician

♦ Consistently fill, secure, and label containers according to customer specifications

♦ Accurately verify goods packaged against package invoices

♦ Carefully adhere to all regulatory guidelines, including execution of supporting product documentation

♦ Regularly maintain the quality of machine output

♦ Follow all applicable waste, scrap reduction, and recycling SOPs (standard operating procedures) without exception

♦ Adhere to safety rules at all times, including wearing appropriate personal protective equipment

♦ Assemble approximately 500 parts per hour with 99% accuracy

♦ Regularly ensure adherence to the quality control plan by following all standard operating procedures

♦ Immediately report any discrepancies in procedures to the area supervisor

♦ Accurately document and check your work for quality and compliance

♦ Operate assigned machinery efficiently and safely

♦ Perform simple maintenance and mechanical assembly as necessary

♦ Report malfunctioning equipment immediately to your supervisor or lead without having to be asked

♦ Continuously monitor products for defects

♦ Follow all applicable safety guidelines, job aids, and policies without exception

♦ Regularly examine paperwork for each product to ensure correct labeling

- ◆ Periodically inspect products for gross visual defects such as color, texture, and debris
- ◆ Never enter the factory floor without wearing personal protective equipment, as required
- ◆ Rotate your responsibilities to learn more about assembly, inspection, and auditing
- ◆ Always maintain a safe and clutter-free work area
- ◆ Submit accurate and timely documentation to comply with FDA regulations
- ◆ Assist other teams with packaging and loading responsibilities when your work slows down
- ◆ Make yourself more available to cross-train on other equipment and in other departments

Equipment Technician

- ◆ Perform all equipment repairs utilizing vendor technical manuals and wiring schematics
- ◆ Regularly ensure that parts received from stock are properly labeled
- ◆ Document your time and supply usage to accurately bill customers
- ◆ Always practice good housekeeping habits (i.e., by keeping your work area clean and hazard free)
- ◆ Keeps your tools and equipment operating in excellent working order
- ◆ Determine whether a part is cost effective to repair or the item should be scrapped before you begin your work
- ◆ Maintain an adequate supply of test fixtures and test units
- ◆ Ensure efficient operations by troubleshooting breakdowns, performing preventive maintenance, and calling for repairs as necessary
- ◆ Perform warranty work in strict accordance with manufacturers' specifications
- ◆ Become more familiar with diagnostic tools, service aids, and product schematics to effectively troubleshoot and resolve equipment and system failures
- ◆ Prioritize repair demands more effectively to ensure optimum customer service
- ◆ Routinely implement preventive maintenance procedures

- Detect errors in defective assemblies, and document your findings consistently
- Demonstrate greater flexibility in providing emergency support for unscheduled maintenance repairs
- Consistently document in the service order the work performed, parts replaced, and tests conducted
- Maintain strong working relationship with vendors
- Provide the master scheduler with daily updates of schedule conflicts and completion of rush orders
- Identify nonconforming, expired shelf-life material for proper disposition
- Provide hot leads to your assigned sales representative for up-selling opportunities
- Attend all training and safety programs offered by equipment manufacturers with appropriate senior management approval
- Update your job knowledge by participating in educational opportunities and reading technical publications
- Remain committed to practicing safety-conscious behaviors in all operational processes and procedures

Master Scheduler

- Successfully maintain the planning and master production schedules
- Regularly review and compare schedule performance against baseline program plans
- Analyze supply and demand at the item, customer, and master schedule levels to determine out-of-balance conditions
- Schedule and release work orders to the production floor in an efficient manner
- Proactively collaborate with program managers to create metrics for process improvement
- Pay greater attention to scheduling parameters, such as lot sizes and lead and cycle times
- Provide management with an understanding of the current schedule's risks and opportunities
- Communicate order status, lead times, and shipping schedules on a timely basis

- Create a concrete plan to address your current challenges with the lack of defined processes, data integrity, and effective information systems
- Investigate new ways to reduce internal lead times as well as lead times to the customer
- Regularly synchronize the master schedule, floor schedule, and shipping schedule
- Summarize daily and weekly master schedules for released orders
- Immediately inform management when demand cannot be met, and recommend alternatives on how the requested demand can be satisfied
- Liaise with the sales department to merge the sales forecast with the manufacturing plan
- Work more closely with engineering to ensure that appropriate labor, machine, and scrap standards are used in master scheduling
- Conduct regular master schedule meetings
- Develop data mining, benchmarking, and predictive analytics to forecast and exceed customer objectives
- Review each master scheduled item at least weekly
- Determine optimal service level and vendor management strategies to achieve customer service and inventory objectives
- Construct data collection, storage, and reporting systems that aid in making sounder procurement-related decisions
- Demonstrate a mastery of manpower, resource, and production planning
- Regularly obtain senior-level management approval for planning agendas
- Pursue your certification in production and inventory management in the upcoming year
- Develop a greater understanding of information systems, order management, and inventory planning tools

Plant Manager

- Develop and execute a plant-specific strategic vision
- Ensure continuous improvement and alignment with your enterprise vision, mission, and objectives

- Coordinate manufacturing schedules based on sales requirements and plant capacity
- Develop and manage the facility budget with a keen eye on capital expenditures and cost management
- Make safety a priority by monitoring lost time accident rates
- Ensure regulatory compliance, with a special focus on OSHA safety standards, FLSA wage and hour compliance, and NLRB collective bargaining rules
- Execute the capital plan in light of the rolling five-year plan
- Drive continuous process/manufacturing improvements in product development and implementation
- Develop a culture of high performance and accountability in employee and product safety
- Work more closely with the corporate team to explore profitable capital investment opportunities
- Perform scheduled audits and inspections of the facility to ensure compliance
- Develop new methods and procedures that create value for the operation by eliminating waste and controlling costs
- Direct project priorities and maintain a master schedule to ensure efficient operations
- Ensure that proper maintenance programs are in place to support the plant's manufacturing assets
- Insist on adherence to administrative and operational policies and procedures
- Regularly execute predictive and preventive maintenance to eliminate catastrophic failures and unplanned maintenance
- Always set and maintain high housekeeping standards
- Display a thorough knowledge of the emergency action plans necessary to comply with the company's disaster recovery and business continuity efforts
- Regularly maintain a plant filing system and control of key operating documents
- Maintain a corrective action system to analyze and correct nonconforming conditions and complaints
- Actively participate in our annual budget and capital expenditure planning process

- Make ongoing operational decisions that adhere to budget requirements and sales goals
- Implement metrics and measurements to effectively evaluate organizational performance trends
- Rely on the enterprise resource planning (ERP) system to quantify and qualify overall production operations
- Assess supplier capabilities and monitor supplier quality to ensure acceptable levels of performance
- Demonstrate greater knowledge of scale-up methods and experimentation planning
- Explore certification by the American Society for Quality (ASQ) as a Certified Quality Engineer (CQE)

Production Supervisor

- Implement measures to improve production methods, equipment performance, and product quality
- Decrease product cost through continuous improvement activities
- Achieve production schedule requirements while operating within established budgetary requirements
- Check raw material availability and designate raw material lot numbers for each batch
- Direct the production of equipment assembly, parts, and components to meet production schedules and quality requirements
- Ensure that all material moves are documented properly
- Verify that clean-outs of tanks and reactors are completed consistently in accordance with documented quality procedures
- Hold regular weekly team meetings covering safety, quality, and reliability issues
- Analyze production schedules more thoroughly to prioritize tasks and reassign resources as needed
- Direct employees in adjusting machines and equipment that fail to meet standards
- Ensure that manpower requirements are met in accordance with the terms outlined in the collective bargaining agreement
- Ensure that quality control checks are carried out according to schedule

- Ensure that correct housekeeping procedures on machinery and in designated work areas are regularly maintained
- Aggressively investigate labor cost variances
- Ensure the highest standards of safety and housekeeping in compliance with company policies and governmental regulations
- Make a greater effort to keep the nightshift informed of production developments
- Develop capital equipment justifications for equipment, tools, and process technology to improve quality, cost, and cycle times
- Analyze work orders to estimate employee hours
- Create equipment-operating schedules that meet both internal and external needs
- Ensure that preventative maintenance requirements are performed according to machine specifications
- Accomplish all production goals in quality, cost, and service while maintaining a safe working environment
- Design systems to evaluate efficiency and compliance in the production area
- Ensure compliance with environmental policies, including hazardous waste management rules
- Develop a strong functional knowledge of Lean manufacturing concepts

Purchasing Agent

- Effectively negotiate prices, terms, delivery, and conditions of purchase from suppliers
- Proactively engage with suppliers to negotiate and resolve performance issues that may impact costs, customer service, or inventory
- Regularly request and analyze bids and approve suppliers
- Implement controls to confirm purchase orders, issue change notices, catalog supplier prices, and prepare quotations
- Ensure that component, standard cost, and lead times are maintained within the system
- Utilize all resources at your disposal to maximize customer service levels and financial performance

- Provide effective inventory forecasts for financial planning
- Provide timely communication on issues that could result in manufacturing or service delays or interruptions
- Effectively coordinate communication between operating departments and suppliers
- Stay on top of purchasing department reports, especially cost reviews, price predictions, effects of material costs on products, and supplier capacity
- Maintain cumulative cost savings and avoidance records to meet the fiscal year budget
- Oversee regular supplier performance reviews, including corrective action and continuous improvement plans
- Maintain timely and accurate order acknowledgments and supplier promise dates
- Maintain a close alliance with the quality assurance department to ensure that suppliers are informed and meeting all product quality, testing, and reporting requirements
- Regularly update the system with delivery information from expediting reports
- Maintain branch purchasing, inventory, and supplier files in a more organized manner
- Expedite open purchase orders to suppliers to maximize stock availability and to ensure the timely delivery of product
- Ensure that suppliers provide delivery confirmation in an accurate and timely manner
- See yourself as a role model for the rest of the company from a purchasing competencies point of view
- Improve service levels and customer satisfaction scores in light of recent survey findings
- Convey a continuous improvement mindset in all matters relating to purchasing materials, components, equipment, and services
- Constructively process and settle claims against suppliers
- Regularly ensure compliance with standard policies and procedures, internal audit, and Sarbanes-Oxley controls
- Visit suppliers' facilities to ensure that their qualifications and capabilities remain current
- Demonstrate a greater knowledge and awareness of industry-leading supply chain methodologies and practices

Quality Assurance Engineer

- Lead problem-solving and root-cause identification efforts
- Effectively guide others in initiating standards and methods for inspection, testing, and evaluation
- Assist in new product qualifications for both product performance and manufacturability
- Tabulate data concerning materials, product, and process in terms of both quality and reliability
- Gather and analyze key metrics data for repair effectiveness and quality
- Lead the corrective action process to ensure that identified causes are adequately addressed
- Guide others in performing specification reviews
- Regularly analyze nonconformances, resolve root causes, and participate in corrective action reports
- Analyze requirements and create tests for developers to use in test-driven development
- Lead continuous improvement teams using Lean and Six Sigma methods
- Execute the complete QA cycle (including functional, system, integration, negative, boundary, and automation) on web applications and batch processes
- Develop forms, instructions, and procedures for evaluating quality and reliability data
- Develop and implement methods and procedures for disposition of discrepant material
- Create audit-finding reports, and determine proper corrective and preventive actions
- Participate in ISO 9001 and AS9100 maintenance activities, including audits, preventative and corrective action, and continuous improvement
- Provide process overview checks to ensure data correctness, completeness, and integrity
- Scope, develop, and execute test plans and test cases for complex, highly scalable, and fault-tolerant systems and interfaces
- Develop training modules to build quality awareness

- Continuously improve the quality control manual and all supporting procedures and work instructions
- Develop plans to drive improvement in key metrics
- Maintain the approved supplier listing, perform supplier audits, and arrange for third-party audits of suppliers
- Conduct audits for incoming materials, in-process, and final inspections
- Analyze failure, corrective, and preventive action to respond to customer complaints
- Ensure the timely resolution of supplier failure, corrective actions, and preventive actions
- Pursue your certification as an internal auditor or lead assessor
- Demonstrate a greater understanding of Lean and Six Sigma philosophies

Supply Chain Manager

- Develop the master schedule to determine the proper lead times of each operation and to meet shipping dates based on customer orders and sales forecasts
- Plan and review requirements for the smallest acceptable inventory levels
- Develop redundant sources as part of an overall business interruption plan
- Assist with the product lifecycle related to returns, exchanges, maintenance releases, and upgrades
- Regularly assess and qualify potential strategic supply partners
- Ensure that each vendor's supply chain is adequately monitored to avoid material interruptions
- Work more closely with sales to complete the timely acknowledgment of orders
- Negotiate and execute favorable strategic purchasing agreements within budgetary limitations
- Work more closely with vendors to determine their cost drivers and lead times
- Provide regular reports on all aspects of the supply chain, including inventory, delivery, and shortages

- Regularly monitor existing supply agreements
- Ensure proper compliance with all legal requirements regarding domestic and international shipments
- Work more aggressively on material cost reductions
- Communicate more regularly with accounting on matters dealing with inventory carrying costs
- Prepare orders and bid requests and negotiate contracts within budget guidelines
- Demonstrate a greater understanding of customer processes for new product introductions, including demand planning, forecasting, and scorecard evaluations
- Assess the ongoing suitability of supply agreements for current and future requirements
- Support new product launches by developing supply and demand plans that support ongoing stocking plans against multiple launch scenarios
- Negotiate global supplier contracts that improve quality, cost, and delivery
- Develop metrics for monitoring supply chain processes and take corrective action for continuous improvement
- Track supplier performance in terms of quality, delivery schedule performance, and price
- Gain a stronger understanding of vendor management, supplier selection, supplier auditing, and supplier lead time reduction
- Develop supply chain strategies for multiple product lines
- Demonstrate a detailed knowledge of supplier capacity constraints, capacity, and shipment schedules

Operations

Administrative Assistant

- Proofread and edit your e-mail before sending
- Answer incoming telephone calls with a greater sense of customer service and willingness to help
- Take accurate and detailed meeting minutes, and regularly follow up with action items
- Prepare correspondence for review by adapting and customizing existing templates
- Demonstrate greater flexibility when responding to last-minute changes in routine
- Become more adept at independently managing small to medium-sized projects
- Strengthen your ability to juggle multiple tasks and projects with competing deadlines
- Increase the overall effectiveness and efficiency of our department by developing a stronger understanding of our processes and systems
- Proactively track and flag renewals that are due to expire within 90 days
- Produce high-quality results under tight deadlines by exercising stronger judgment and common sense when prioritizing your work
- Escalate nonroutine matters as appropriate in order to resolve issues effectively
- Ensure that appointments are kept within the allotted time and time management conflicts are avoided

♦ Demonstrate a greater awareness of communicating effectively in a multicultural environment with diverse backgrounds and lifestyles

♦ Make travel arrangements, prepare travel itineraries, and process travel reimbursements smoothly and seamlessly

♦ Develop a stronger understanding of the workflow in our department and knowledge of common business terminology

♦ Provide temporary backup support to other administrative team members without hesitation

♦ Become more involved in supervising and overseeing the part-time office assistant

♦ Draft responses for routine correspondence and regularly recurring requests

♦ Regularly verify that incoming invoices are billed appropriately and coded properly for payment

♦ Ensure that filing, faxing, copying, and incoming mail are administered consistently and in a timely fashion

♦ Communicate any time you are falling behind in your work or otherwise suspect that you may miss a deadline, so that other resources can be deployed

♦ Always ensure that proper room and/or dial-in arrangements are made for videoconferences

♦ Demonstrate greater independence in your role by answering routine inquiries without further consultation

♦ Account for any missed breaks or meal periods when entering your weekly timekeeping report

♦ Demonstrate flexibility to work unscheduled overtime when the need arises

♦ Serve as liaison/ambassador for our department by graciously welcoming visitors and helping them find their way around our facility

♦ Focus on improving your organizational skills so that you can locate necessary documents on short notice

♦ Eliminate rework by double-checking your materials before submitting them to others

♦ Avoid appearing to resist requests to answer others' phones when necessary

♦ Become a reliable resource on questions about office procedures and protocol

Customer Service Representative

♦ Recognize the value of your role as a key player in every stage of the business, from managing customers and processing orders to coordinating product delivery

♦ Always provide friendly service and enthusiastic sales guidance to customers

♦ Do a better job of keeping merchandise in excellent, rent-ready condition

♦ Consistently secure on-time payments and collect on delinquent accounts

♦ Readily assist in maintaining our quality showroom without being asked

♦ Rapidly investigate errant shipments and shortage inquiries

♦ Demonstrate strong listening skills and present products on a problem-to-solution basis

♦ Readily distinguish between features and benefits when cross-selling opportunities arise

♦ Respond to all customer requests for information on a timely basis

♦ Become technically proficient on equipment operated and maintained by your assigned customers

♦ Identify and act on opportunities to create new sales opportunities

♦ Identify, implement, and improve on processes that make it easier for customers to do business with your company

♦ Find new ways of enhancing customers' sales and purchasing satisfaction

♦ Prepare and manage quotes and sales orders throughout the product life cycle, ensuring that nothing falls through the cracks

♦ Demonstrate stronger project management skills, especially in terms of managing multiple projects simultaneously

♦ Provide accurate and timely order entry and price quotations

♦ Demonstrate a greater customer orientation in terms of lending an empathetic ear when fielding questions and facing objections

♦ Ensure that all customer and sales records are up-to-date and in compliance with the company's record retention policy

♦ Always gain advance permission for amended orders

- Demonstrate a greater awareness and knowledge of product availability and price, invoice status, shipment dates, and pending claims
- Display a stronger concern for quality and accuracy in your work
- Strengthen your reputation for your listening, understanding, and responding ability
- Demonstrate a willingness to support the credit/finance department in the resolution of sales order credit and financial hold issues
- Understand the critical role you play in exceeding customer expectations
- Always focus on expanding sales while helping to ensure a smooth and efficient transaction experience
- View every customer service transaction as an opportunity to build loyalty and trust
- Significantly reduce your percentage of order entry errors when documenting product numbers and change orders
- Develop a stronger performance track record for upselling additional products
- Obtain stronger customer satisfaction and quality control scorecard results
- Strengthen your skills in promotional product selling
- Present more of a can-do attitude when being challenged by emotional customers who appear to be unwilling or unable to listen to reason
- Determine what steps you'll need to take to advance into an assistant store manager position

Dispatcher

- Regularly assess capacity and equipment requirements to determine the best method of transportation
- Monitor the dispatch board throughout the day, and adjust routes as necessary
- Maximize service technicians' productivity by setting predetermined sales stops to fill up an entire day
- Resolve all transportation challenges with a sense of urgency and professionalism

- Promptly place outbound calls to customers for preappointment verification, outage resolution, and work order cancellation
- Proactively monitor job pools by rescheduling unfilled time slots and overbookings
- Fine-tune and adjust technician routes during the span of the day to respond to fluctuations in demand and to minimize drive times
- Create efficient schedules for all drivers by minimizing rerouting activities
- Propose tentative schedules by 3:00 P.M., and confirm the official schedule by 5:00 P.M. each day
- Accurately calculate the information required to bill customer invoices
- Regularly follow up with customers once the job is finished to confirm work completion and to gauge customer satisfaction
- Negotiate rates in light of market, capacity, and location considerations
- Proactively schedule all vehicles for their regular service, general maintenance, and necessary repairs
- Spread work more evenly across the driver base
- Create purchase orders for parts and materials needed for daily service work and for service contracts
- Verbally confirm with all drivers the location of their first stop for the following morning
- Set schedules according to the type of load being hauled, Department of Transportation (DOT) safety requirements, the availability of equipment, and delivery deadlines
- Utilize the call list and duty roster to track driver acceptance of loads
- Show greater flexibility with rerouting in light of truck breakdowns, weather conditions, or safety service incidents
- Regularly communicate ETAs (estimated times of arrival) and location updates with customers and field personnel
- Accurately record run information for origin and destination, including truck and trailer numbers
- Apply for permits for overweight or oversize loads in a timely manner
- Ensure that all driver vehicle inspection reports, driver logs, and delivery bills are completed accurately and on time
- Make recommendations to improve overall routing effectiveness

♦ Diligently modify work orders to reflect customer changes, system outages, and route interruptions

♦ Develop a greater understanding of the ancillary equipment used to support your company's vehicles

♦ Become more fluent with the mobile resource management tools available to effectively manage technicians' arrival times and shift completions

♦ Demonstrate a greater knowledge of DOT regulations and multistate geography

Facilities Maintenance Supervisor

♦ Establish and recommend priorities on repair projects and estimate their cost

♦ Ensure that your team corrects equipment problems that cause excessive production downtime

♦ Determine root-cause failures to identify and correct chronic equipment problems

♦ Maintain and analyze equipment data and history records to better predict maintenance needs

♦ Keep current on preventive maintenance procedures based on manufacturers' recommendations

♦ Conduct a variety of maintenance services to ensure the availability and performance of all equipment and building systems

♦ Communicate production challenges and delays in a timely fashion

♦ Ensure that our facility operates under safe conditions according to established policies and procedures and in compliance with federal, state, county, and municipal regulations

♦ Maintain local spare parts as well as tools and equipment in excellent working order

♦ Replenish inventories of replacement parts and components with a keen eye on budget restrictions

♦ Establish a min/max program that identifies the quantities that should be warehoused to run operations efficiently and improve daily productivity

♦ Propose changes to the annual capital and operating expense budgets to support the maintenance of facility equipment and systems

♦ Calculate the return on investment (ROI) for project justifications and proposed capital expenditures

♦ Become more knowledgeable regarding building code and regulatory compliance issues

♦ Track and maintain certificates of occupancy, occupant safety, and compliance (that is, heating, ventilation, and air conditioning as well as fire, elevator, and OSHA)

♦ Demonstrate sufficient local knowledge of operations to ensure the efficient and effective operation of the facility and systems

♦ Develop emergency procedures and identify essential maintenance personnel ready to assist in emergencies

♦ Serve as an active member of our business continuity/disaster planning team

♦ Develop your team to handle a wider variety of challenges, including equipment failures, weather-related actions, and security incidents

♦ Enhance your understanding of the computerized maintenance management system

♦ Obtain sufficient price quotes for needed repairs

♦ Update and maintain all spare parts and replacement schedules when new equipment or systems are installed

♦ Strengthen your technical knowledge of production, mechanical, and electrical equipment

♦ Develop more flexible capabilities in the general trades, including electrical and motor circuitry, plumbing and piping, and workplace ergonomics and safety

Office Manager

♦ Oversee and support company operations by diligently managing and directing all administrative office support functions

♦ Assume full responsibility for all aspects of day-to-day office operations

♦ Coordinate billing, administration, credit and collections, vendor management, and financial oversight collaboratively and seamlessly

♦ Readily assist with the implementation of short-term and long-range plans based on company goals and growth objectives

- Actively resolve concerns, questions, and complaints raised by vendors, employees, clients, and management
- Prepare guidelines for proper coding of invoices to general ledger expense accounts
- Supervise the matching of invoices with purchase orders and receiving documents
- Negotiate the purchase of office supplies and equipment with a keen eye on budget restrictions
- Pay greater attention to tracking all office supply inventory
- Focus on building your leadership and communication skills to motivate team members and create higher employee satisfaction and engagement
- Develop a jack-of-all-trades approach to juggling multiple tasks with competing deadlines and priorities
- Regularly ensure a high level of staff performance
- Approve employee time entry for payroll hours, ensuring that all overtime worked and skipped breaks or meal periods are accurately reflected
- Flag all employee expense reimbursement requests or accounts payable invoices that are outside budget guidelines
- Regularly assist facilities management with janitorial, landscaping, and general property upkeep projects
- Ensure the timely and accurate preparation of journals, general ledger entries, and budget reports
- Do not formally close the monthly books until all variances are accounted for
- Demonstrate greater accuracy in reconciling receipts and disbursements
- Consistently ensure that accounting records are kept in accordance with state and federal laws and in preparation for periodic financial audits
- Advance your technical skills in QuickBooks by enrolling in an appropriate online course by the end of the first quarter
- Regularly assist HR in the hiring process, especially with initial applicant screening and testing
- Construct action templates that others could easily follow in your absence
- Actively monitor petty cash funds to ensure we have enough on hand to cover ordinary expenses

♦ Ensure that all matters relating to equipment maintenance and repair are resolved on a timely basis

♦ Immediately escalate any issues that can impact payroll or compliance standards

Receptionist

♦ Screen and answer incoming telephone calls in a polite and friendly manner

♦ Hold yourself accountable for creating the initial impression of the company with all visitors, clients, and job prospects

♦ Greet anyone entering the building with a friendly and warm smile

♦ Screen anyone entering the building according to our security and safety guidelines before granting access

♦ Notify employees of visitors' arrivals immediately to avoid confusion

♦ Screen calls aggressively, allowing no one through unless the caller requests the name of a specific employee

♦ Ensure that deliveries do not come through the main lobby and use the proper delivery entrance

♦ Don't leave callers on hold for more than 30 seconds

♦ Accept business cards from solicitors, but do not provide the names of employees without advance permission

♦ Keep abreast of staff movements in and out of the organization

♦ Respond to basic public and customer queries without feeling the need to escalate calls to others

♦ Immediately escalate all calls from government agencies or subpoena deliveries to our legal department before responding

♦ Tidy and maintain the reception area on a regular and proactive basis

♦ Be careful not to leave your workstation often or appear to fraternize with coworkers when you're on duty

♦ Strengthen your knowledge of customer service principles and practices

♦ Understand that your customer service orientation and professional personal presentation go hand in hand with creating an overall impression of the company

◆ Confidently answer visitors' inquiries about the company and its products and services

◆ Look for opportunities to assume bookkeeping and cashiering responsibilities when the front desk gets slow

◆ Readily assume security guard access control functions by verifying employee identification and issuing visitor passes

◆ Immediately report any unusual or suspicious persons or activities in the lobby

◆ Always maintain a calm, courteous, and professional demeanor regardless of a visitor's behavior

◆ Avoid casual or cute expressions like "Honey," "Doll," or "Sweetie" when dealing with visitors or employees

◆ Reduce the number of incoming calls that go to voice mail

◆ Notify your supervisor any time your deskwork slows down so that he or she can assign additional responsibilities to you

◆ Demonstrate stronger organizational forecasting abilities by planning for scheduled vendor deliveries and visitor rush hour trends

◆ Always remain aware of standing management meetings and offsite gatherings to better navigate schedule change requests

◆ Respect confidentiality, and exercise discretion at all times

◆ Recognize the stressful nature of your role in terms of dealing with demanding personalities and coordinating multiple tasks on a last moment's notice

◆ Know that the two key attributes of the receptionist role are a positive attitude and dependability

◆ Proactively manage the scheduling of the boardroom and common conference area

◆ Provide identification cards and arrange for visitor escorts on a timely basis

Research Analyst

◆ Design and manage assigned research projects from conception to completion

◆ Identify, troubleshoot, correct, and/or escalate data issues and irregularities on a timely basis

◆ Demonstrate greater attention to detail and a sharper eye for discrepancies

- Take full ownership of customizing market share analysis reports
- Strengthen your ability to manipulate large data sets
- Develop and maintain forecasting and segmentation models for analyzing spending by industry and by company size
- Recommend and implement new processes and tools for enhancing industry data analysis
- Improve your Excel skills, focusing primarily on your ability to design, develop, and maintain large forecasting models
- Take additional coursework focusing on standard statistical analysis methods (especially regression analysis and data correlations)
- Demonstrate a greater awareness of emerging technologies, the evolving media environment, consumer behavior, and overall economic conditions
- Prepare effective survey instruments and discussion guides in layman's terms
- Make yourself available to work longer and more flexible hours when facing project deadlines
- Demonstrate a greater understanding of business research and analysis, including survey design, data collection, and report design
- Design and manage statistical programs that track production, sales, inventory, and capacity in a wider variety of industries
- Provide research insights and identify targeting opportunities to aid marketing and new business development efforts
- Strengthen your ability to synthesize both quantitative and qualitative sources of data into your forecasting recommendations
- Regularly analyze data from syndicated and proprietary tools to assess current market conditions
- Build stronger and more collaborative relationships with industry experts
- Strengthen your ability to perform complex analytical work using advanced research methodologies
- Demonstrate a greater willingness to work collaboratively in a team environment and creatively under tight deadlines
- Transfer customer feedback into actionable recommendations
- Establish and maintain rapport with diverse demographic groups, including management, professional, technical, and administrative coworkers

Safety and Security Manager

♦ Build an effective safety and security program to reduce risks, respond to incidents, reduce liability, and control losses

♦ Conduct internal and external safety audits and inspections according to schedule

♦ Ensure that you are regularly available on-call 24/7 by phone (home, cell, and pager) for emergency response

♦ Oversee and evaluate all security training and compliance programs

♦ Spearhead the development and review of safety and security policies, practices, and procedures

♦ Review and approve vendor proposals, installations, and repairs on a timely basis

♦ Perform ongoing safety and security assessments, inspections, and audits to ensure compliance with regulatory requirements

♦ Develop new content and updates for the corporate safety and security webpage

♦ Find new and creative ways of contributing to the ongoing development and continuous improvement of safety and security programs

♦ Create a safety and security infrastructure that accounts for all personnel, resources, and assets

♦ Ensure that all facilities are well maintained and provide a safe working environment

♦ Effectively manage all aspects of contract security services, including contract negotiations and contract compliance

♦ Regularly ensure appropriate safety and security staffing levels

♦ Clearly define the budget and scope of work before approving the installation of security system projects

♦ Readily partner with law enforcement officials in the completion of investigations

♦ Demonstrate greater proficiency using our incident reporting system, particularly with incident-investigation and report-writing procedures

♦ Proactively anticipate security program needs, and set priorities accordingly

♦ Ensure that safety and security objectives are specific, measurable, scheduled, and completed

◆ Provide safety and security consultation to management, committees, workgroups, and others

◆ Carefully track and trend incident reporting and patrol tour statistical reporting

◆ Establish goals, work activities, and accountabilities in light of new and existing safety and security requirements

◆ Develop and document the methods needed to ensure compliance with policies, procedures, governmental regulations, state mandates, and local ordinances

◆ Fine-tune your experience working with card access systems and contract security services

◆ Obtain professional certification as a Certified Protection Professional through the American Society for Industrial Security within 24 months

◆ Audit company facilities, and make remedial recommendations to comply with OSHA, federal, state, and local regulations

◆ Meet all budget guidelines by tracking expenses and obtaining at least three competitive bids on all capital improvement projects

◆ Maintain your personal certification in first aid, CPR, and bloodborne pathogens

◆ Serve as the departmental lead on all business continuity planning (BCP) and disaster planning initiatives

Transportation Manager

◆ Effectively oversee all aspects of fleet maintenance, including supervision of dispatchers and drivers, staffing, training, and support for warehouse operations

◆ Make regular site visits to ensure safe, efficient, and profitable field operations

◆ Guide the transportation team to build and deliver continuous enhancements in service and cost

◆ Regularly monitor driver safety, and take proactive steps to create a positive safety culture

◆ Conduct a quarterly profit and loss (P&L) analysis to determine trends in costs and to maximize profitability

◆ Ensure that customer billing and employee payroll are accurate and timely

- Collaborate with distribution center managers and plant materials managers to develop integrated cost and service goals
- Complete and submit incident reports within 24 hours
- Continuously evaluate standard operating procedures, business rules, and work processes to enhance communication and streamline efficiencies
- Regularly identify discrepancies in fuel card usage patterns or odometer readings
- Spend more time on-site with your customers and learn the ins and outs of their yard management systems
- Be safety conscious at all times, and report safety questions and concerns immediately (never later than 24 hours)
- Ensure that the team is completing pre- and post-trip inspections on all equipment
- Analyze and report on key performance indicators and metrics when preparing budgets and forecasts
- Direct the transportation team to monitor carrier costs and service performance, including reliability and responsiveness rates as well as carrier loss and damage claims
- Collaborate with customer service to develop multifunctional plans that improve service, cost, and customer satisfaction
- Optimize the company's assets by monitoring revenue and costs through effective profit and loss (P&L) analysis
- Strengthen your working knowledge of supply chain management and transportation logistics
- Demonstrate a clearer understanding of contribution margin statements and of line-haul and back-haul reports
- Consistently ensure compliance with company policies and federal Department of Transportation (DOT) regulations

Warehouse Manager

- Ensure optimum order process management for receiving, storage, packing, and shipping
- Drive continuous process improvement throughout all functions of the warehouse
- Regularly ensure that company procedures and regulations are followed with regard to sanitation, storage, and safety

+ Diligently set and manage capital projects
+ Constantly look for new opportunities to identify cost-saving improvements and increased efficiencies
+ Accurately manage the inventory of goods using the appropriate FIFO (first-in/first-out) inventory management procedure techniques
+ Demonstrate greater hands-on involvement in managing the company's high-volume, fast-paced warehouse/distribution center
+ Coordinate appropriate and timely operational training as necessary
+ Manage operational expenses, including labor and supplies, in order to meet or exceed budgetary expectations
+ Carefully manage and preserve all documentation for three 24/7 shift assignments
+ Continually evaluate production and quality standards to affect continued improvement in overall performance
+ Provide greater oversight of physical inventory, including cycle counts and adjustments
+ Maintain accurate operational records, including the preparation of building and safety audits that support our health and safety plan
+ Communicate job expectations clearly, and carefully monitor results
+ Facilitate effective communication among members of the supervisory and management team, between shifts, and between management and hourly employees
+ Demonstrate greater support for employee morale-building events such as holiday parties and company picnics
+ Create accurate daily work logs, and audit daily labor and billing reports
+ Redefine the workflow and set work schedules to ensure that orders are processed accurately and timely according to company protocol
+ Maintain the facility to ensure that it is clean, orderly, operational, and free of debris
+ Regularly ensure that all warehouse employees maintain a safe and clean working environment
+ Develop and enforce safety processes to meet OSHA requirements without exception
+ Address problem situations head-on when appraising job results, coaching, counseling, and disciplining employees
+ Synthesize data trends to develop appropriate work-related directives for your team

- Regularly maintain and issue the inventory report, entry and exit status report, dead stock report, goods age report, consumption report, and manpower status report

- Document your efforts at implementing cost reduction measures in all aspects of warehouse transaction activities

- Demonstrate an in-depth understanding of all facets of contemporary distribution operations

- Pursue Six Sigma and Lean manufacturing certification to better meet the needs of your role

- Develop greater familiarity with your warehouse management system proprietary software

Sales, Marketing, and Digital Media

Account Executive

- Effectively manage the entire sales cycle from prospecting to creative deal solution to client onboarding
- Properly qualify business opportunities up front before investing in new relationships
- Develop sales proposals, estimates, specifications, and presentations that focus on long-term contract renewal and revenue expansion opportunities
- Set the appropriate number of sales activities to meet performance targets
- Aggressively generate revenue from new sales and renewals through cold calling and online sales presentations
- Close sufficient business to meet monthly, quarterly, and annual sales objectives
- Develop and deploy sound account development strategies that allow you to maximize your profit-per-deal ratios
- Avoid chasing high-activity, low-margin business
- Find a healthier balance between your new business development initiatives and account maintenance activities
- Pursue sound business opportunities that permit sustained customer satisfaction and promote long-term relationships
- Track the quality ratios of sales calls to maximize each territory's potential
- Provide outstanding, proactive service to your assigned client base to generate a higher renewal ratio on existing sales
- Think relationship first, transaction second

- Engage in consultative selling techniques that provide recommendations on a problem-to-solution basis even if you don't get the sale
- Create and adhere to a well-researched client development plan
- Maintain cooperative working relationships with all necessary departments to ensure that new sales are properly processed and quickly activated
- Conduct periodic postsale, quality assurance visits to ensure client satisfaction
- Assist in resolving installation roadblocks to ensure a smooth handover to the account maintenance team
- Periodically invite clients from different industries to lunch to help them develop stronger networks with their peers
- Proactively identify current and future customer service requirements
- Prepare accurate and thorough sales activity and expense tracking reports
- Keep current on market and product trends to strengthen your reputation as a subject matter expert in the field
- Provide creative and insightful one-off solutions to your clients only after securing advanced corporate approval
- Continue to pursue in-depth product and service knowledge, and acquire deeper selling, technical, and financial skills
- Secure profitable, high-margin business that achieves your booking and gross margin goals
- Strengthen your retention and repeat-business ratios

Digital Content Producer

- Produce engaging, fresh, and original content that encourages customers to interact with the company website
- Create and develop more compelling and original content to enhance the company's online presence
- Develop consumer-relevant content that highlights brand products, contests, promotions, events, and partnerships
- Accurately write, proofread, and edit copy for e-mail, site, and social network placement
- Regularly track the online retail landscape for content and campaign ideas that will drive ecommerce goals

- Confirm accurate product data entry and error/expectation management on data feeds
- Perform extensive analysis on keywords, and manage the keyword portfolio to ensure optimal product placement on the site
- Produce effective product content for digital marketing assets and partner websites
- Review and evaluate web analytics reports to trend and forecast website consumer behavior
- Generate variations in content for multiple consumer segments
- Examine website product catalog traffic to determine new product purchases, features, and promotions
- Uphold established site and e-mail style guides without exception
- Regularly assign product to style categories, cross-sell/up-sell features, and customer search queries
- Readily assist the ecommerce marketing managers with content and functionality testing
- Provide social media and blog content recommendations based on e-commerce revenue drivers
- Secure brand approvals for all content prior to delivery or placement
- Ensure that content is consistent and linked across multiple consumer touch points, including e-mail, online advertising, and brand websites
- Demonstrate greater creativity and originality in developing and coordinating product, customer-generated, and online merchandising content
- Work closely with IT to implement content upgrades and to ensure technical feasibility
- Ensure that all published content consistently adheres to overall site design and technical standards
- Use consumer insights and brand data to understand consumer personas by brand
- Oversee SEO (search engine optimization) practices, including HTML page construction, site architecture, and content and keyword research
- Demonstrate a strengthened understanding of basic HTML and web analytics tools
- Strengthen your knowledge of emerging web technologies and digital media, including content, networking, searches, and web marketing

Digital Marketing Manager

♦ Effectively drive the overall digital marketing strategy for your core brands

♦ Create a world-class corporate website that aligns with your brand and delivers fresh, insightful content in a way that inspires visitors to action

♦ Provide strategic guidance recommendations for all of the company's digital media plans

♦ Establish benchmarks, champion best practices, and educate brand teams on forward-looking digital activation possibilities

♦ Constantly look for opportunities to develop new websites for newly identified markets

♦ Identify new strategies, tactics, and technologies to ensure competitiveness in the digital marketing space

♦ Establish the global standards for web design, architecture, messaging, and content

♦ Implement a web strategy that results in improved lead generation, increased site traffic, and enhanced customer experience

♦ Work more collaboratively with the marketing team to create digital activation concepts

♦ Always keep the technological capabilities of customer usability in mind when testing website navigability and developing web design

♦ Provide recommendations for optimizing the user experience on company websites

♦ Ensure that your team exercises a unique blend of strategic thinking, creativity, technical proficiency, and operational excellence

♦ Investigate the optimum utilization of social media for customer and prospect interaction

♦ Develop meaningful performance metrics that drive appropriate sales results and traffic to our customer care site

♦ Define the key performance indicators to measure success and return on investment (ROI)

♦ Integrate the latest technical and marketing tools to drive site traffic and to convert visitors to leads

♦ Remain current on digital marketing best practices with regard to search engine optimization (SEO), publishing strategies, campaign analysis, and CAN-SPAM compliance (Controlling the Assault of Non-Solicited Pornography and Marketing Act of 2003, the law governing commercial e-mail distribution to customers)

- Improve revenue from e-mail through systematic testing, analysis, and optimization
- Partner with IT in leading the selection and implementation of e-mail systems and platforms
- Maximize the website user experience by focusing on user engagement and site consistency
- Prepare and present postprogram reports on digital activity every week
- Regularly collect and analyze website data, and perform market and competitive analysis to forecast critical trends in usage patterns
- Lead the strategy development and execution for all e-mail marketing campaigns to support conversion, usage, and retention across your product range
- Work more closely with marketing to integrate current e-initiatives with existing offline efforts
- Demonstrate a more thorough understanding of e-mail best practices with regard to campaign analysis, deliverability and segmentation strategies, and HTML e-mail rendering and design
- Enforce a consistent and holistic strategy, style, and voice across all platforms
- Ensure that your team has a keen understanding of Internet marketing practices, website development, search engine marketing, and search engine optimization principles
- Identify and establish strategic content partnerships
- Keep abreast of the latest Internet trends, business models, social media policies, and web/search engine optimization (SEO) technologies

Field Sales Representative

- Make regular sales calls to designated on-premise accounts to cultivate customer relations and to heighten satisfaction with company services
- Generate a minimum of three sales per week in your local market via onsite meetings
- Manage and grow your assigned territory by actively soliciting referrals from satisfied customers
- Conduct territory analysis to target top prospects with the highest return potential

- Build immediate rapport and cultivate relationships with customers who may not initially recognize the need for your services
- Overcome objections in a caring but compelling way
- Establish common grounds and focus on win-win outcomes
- Draft scripts to address your three most common objections and the ways you've overcome them
- Effectively qualify prospects to avoid investing too much time in so-called Lookie Lou's
- Differentiate your sales strategy for prospecting new accounts, retaining existing accounts, and up-selling promotional products to existing customers
- Address customer concerns with an eye on moving the customer toward commitment
- Demonstrate consultative selling abilities by listening closely to customer needs and acting as a customer advocate and voice
- Promote new and existing portfolio items that meet existing customers' specialized needs
- Exhibit discipline and resourcefulness to meet and exceed assigned monthly quotas and performance objectives
- Develop and sustain strong customer relationships with key decision makers
- Readily assist customers with inventory management responsibilities (i.e., product placement and rotation of stock)
- Report daily on your sales progress and attainment of goals
- Increase your proficiency in calculating commissions and analyzing comparative sales data
- Negotiate competitive contract rates to increase your profitability-per-deal ratio
- Readily share market and competitor information with all applicable channels within the organization
- Develop a stronger understanding of the solutions that your products provide
- Keep up with industry trends and developments to strengthen your conversational communication skills
- Frequently attend area trade shows and industry events
- Develop strong relations within the sales department and with cross-functional support teams

- Find creative and compelling ways to drive new sales opportunities within your defined territory
- Organize and present sales reports and quota attainment results at the end of each week
- Resolve missing or incomplete information, and account for anomalies and inconsistencies before submitting sales orders
- Manage your multistate territory in a cost-effective manner by minimizing redundant travel and entertainment costs

Fundraising/Development Executive (Nonprofit)

- Develop effective strategies for donor engagement and the solicitation of top prospects
- Research, identify, and cultivate individual, corporate, and foundation donors
- Devise and implement strategies for donor cultivation
- Drive the necessary development efforts to meet your organization's annual revenue goals
- Create and manage a portfolio with an emphasis on corporations and individual giving
- Develop strategies to approach large multinational corporations regarding national gifts
- Maximize opportunities for cultivating and soliciting major individual, corporate, and institutional donors
- Ensure that your staff consistently prepares gift acknowledgments for all donations
- Develop database systems to track and monitor donor and prospect histories
- Regularly analyze the cost-effectiveness of the company's planned giving program
- Establish an annual fundraising event to support the endowment fund
- Secure funding through the timely submissions of well-researched fundraising proposals and grant requests
- Develop recognition programs that encourage donor renewal and upgrade

- Identify and cultivate major donor prospects from the annual giving donor base
- Develop and maintain ongoing relationships with major donors via personal solicitation
- Identify prospects for cultivation, solicitation, and stewardship of upper-level annual gifts
- Review the giving history of prospects and suspects in order to recommend appropriate solicitation levels
- Develop and execute the annual fundraising plan
- Secure financial support from individuals, foundations, and corporations with knowledge of available community resources
- Manage the implementation of the donor database, and oversee the staff responsible for data entry and gift processing
- Oversee the writing of letters of inquiry, proposals, and other funding requests for submission to individual, corporate, and foundation donors and prospects
- Work closely with the board of directors to achieve established short- and long-term fundraising revenue goals
- Recommend well-justified annual goals and budget projections
- Oversee donor communications, including collateral print and marketing materials used in the cultivation and solicitation of individual and corporate donors
- Forge stronger relationships with key corporate and civic community leaders
- Make personal solicitation visits to alumni and other key prospective donors at least once per quarter
- Hire, direct, and develop community directors in the areas of fundraising, volunteer development, planning, and budgeting
- Work collaboratively with volunteers on events and solicitations
- Recruit, train, and motivate an extensive volunteer network to assist in annual fundraising activities

Grant Writer (Nonprofit)

- Conduct targeted research on the availability of private and government funds
- Proactively identify new or previously untapped potential funding sources

- Creatively identify potential funding sources that match program development goals
- Conduct thorough research on every potential grant, including lists of previous grantees, project summaries, successful applications, and relevant web resources
- Expand your network of key city, county, state, and federal personnel to support your grant-writing efforts
- Create compelling and accurate grant proposals in line with your organizational philosophy
- Exhibit strong expository writing skills when drafting grant applications
- Ensure that written proposals include accurate program descriptions and pricing
- Develop long-range plans that support identified program priorities when submitting grant applications for funding
- Establish and maximize productive relationships with content and program specialists as resources for accurate text development
- Provide clear guidance to authors on proposal content and graphics development
- Collaborate more closely with the program staff to develop proposal goals and with finance for budget preparation
- Finalize applications in compliance with funder requirements
- Submit draft applications to the review team at least one week in advance of the due date
- Regularly ensure that proposals are ready for scheduled reviews and final delivery within the established deadlines
- Thoroughly review the budget of a funding project or program before recommending it to the proposal committee
- Ensure that all necessary forms, signatures, approvals, and other ancillary materials are included in each proposal package
- Demonstrate an increasingly effective ability to work with more than one client at a time and to balance multiple projects and applications
- Maintain internal materials in the current proposal library without exception
- Organize all relevant contact information, boilerplate language, and funder information in a centralized file for future reference
- Coordinate all aspects of the submission processes for approved proposals

- Always ensure that the appropriate stakeholders review and approve proposal text
- Strengthen your track record of negotiating and closing major gifts
- Use proposal technology tools and platforms more effectively
- Obtain your professional grant writer certification in the upcoming year

Product/Brand Manager

- Manage the entire product life cycle from strategic planning to tactical activities
- Research markets and your competitors to determine appropriate product positioning
- Specify requirements for current and future products by collaborating with subject matter experts, sales, and external customers
- Build best-of-breed products on time and on spec
- Serve as the go-to person for all product functional questions
- Focus on developing strategies that impact the direction of future products
- Work more closely with the design team to define product vision, direction, and positioning
- Set pricing and manage costs to meet revenue and profitability goals
- Compose requirements and specs that are based on independent, negotiable, and testable user stories
- Drive superior customer experience across all delivery channels
- Regularly budget and track the marketing spend
- Develop creative approaches to communicate brand attributes and to drive consumer behavior
- Regularly utilize metrics to measure results and to adjust your strategy
- Clearly define product positioning and messaging before recommending a go-to-market strategy
- Define your market in terms of customer needs analysis and buyer behavior patterns
- Offer feedback to the product management team regarding new product requirements and future strategy

- Maintain a constant awareness of project deliverables
- Provide ongoing support, guidance, and direction to the project team throughout the project life cycle
- Develop a greater awareness of markets, asset classes, and the competitive landscape
- Identify and resolve issues that may impact project deliverables and time lines
- Establish key consumer insights utilizing appropriate qualitative and quantitative research methods
- Help execute beta tests and pilot programs
- Become an expert in the market relative to the competition, category trends, and share position
- Ensure that products remain true to their design intent

Sales Associate (Retail)

- Look for new and creative methods to establish and maintain customer engagement
- Develop lasting customer relationships through effective clientele-building practices
- Display a higher level of ownership, accountability, and initiative that exceeds customer expectations
- Always ensure that customers receive a distinctive brand experience
- Make world-class customer service your hallmark for building strong customer relationships
- Go out of your way to share your love for the customers you serve, the merchandise you sell, and the work you do
- Demonstrate an enthusiastic and positive attitude when meeting and interacting with clients
- Regularly educate customers on related products, features, and services
- Provide consumer counseling sessions, including product information clinics, promotional events, and in-aisle consumer education
- Effectively merchandise in-store products, including seasonal resets; shelf, rack, and display restocking; and repairing or removing damaged items
- Demonstrate a greater creative flair for arranging products in an attractive manner

- Provide critical market feedback to the store manager regarding local competition and product and service needs
- Take increased advantage of cross-selling and up-selling opportunities
- Maintain a more comprehensive knowledge of all company products, accessories, pricing plans, promotions, and service features
- Demonstrate a greater awareness of store products and services to build sales
- Complete all aspects of opening and closing the store in accordance with established procedures
- Proactively minimize clutter and ensure that merchandise fixtures are organized and fully stocked
- Demonstrate greater flexibility and dependability with scheduling, including nights and weekends
- Consistently handle all administrative aspects of the sale, including completing customer contracts and warranties, pulling products from inventory, and filing completed orders
- Consistently adhere to all loss prevention control and compliance procedures

Social Media Coordinator

- Actively track and analyze website and social media performance
- Create and implement a social media marketing strategy to increase visibility, drive traffic, and increase sales
- Track, analyze, and report on the success of online campaigns
- Immerse yourself more fully in the digital world of communication marketing, social networking, blogging, and online communities
- Develop a comprehensive social media marketing plan for magazines and events
- Strengthen our online reputation by developing social media strategies that grow audiences and build active social communities
- Proactively analyze press coverage, and conduct online research in support of all communications initiatives
- See yourself as a brand ambassador for the company in online communities
- Develop new partnerships to increase online traffic and to maintain strong industry relationships

- Serve as our in-house subject matter expert on social media policies and guidelines
- Craft creative blog entries, blog replies, tweets, and status updates that capture the public's imagination and get the media's attention
- Develop, manage, and track offline and online merchandise sales, fulfillment, and inventory
- Research and recommend best practices for corporate social media engagement
- Contribute regularly to communications strategy sessions, and generate ideas to increase the creativity, persuasive influence, and overall impact of the company's social media message
- Expand and maintain the customer e-mail database
- Work more closely with brand managers to outline and implement website and social media opportunities
- Assume responsibility for planning the monthly social media calendar
- Become more vocal in terms of recommending new social media tools, sites, and apps as part of the social media mix
- Enhance social media outlets and opportunities to build the company's online fan base
- Protect the company's brand by ensuring that positive messaging is maintained in all social media communities
- Manage online discussions by listening to what users are saying, reading discussion forums, and responding in a timely manner to users' needs
- Become more adept at quickly crafting short, compelling copy in an authentic voice that resonates with your target audience
- Demonstrate a greater understanding of the domain name system and IP addressing
- Strengthen your knowledge of search engine optimization (SEO) keyword research and of Google

Telemarketer

- Rely on your daily planner to plan your work and work your plan
- Find new and creative ways of establishing immediate rapport with prospects

- Complete 20 calls per hour and generate a minimum of three to six qualified sales leads per week

- Effectively target clients by researching, prospecting, and nurturing a target list of named accounts

- Seek detailed qualification information to generate strong, high-probability leads

- Make a thorough determination of whether the lead fits the profile of a customer we want to do business with

- Qualify the prospective customer more thoroughly before escalating the call to the Tier 2 business development agents

- Develop new approaches and strategies for delivering compelling presentations

- Demonstrate excellent telephone presence with professionalism, good diction, and enthusiasm

- Present service package options accurately by adhering to the sales script

- Initiate calls to potential clients without veering from the prepared selling script

- Exhibit creativity and good judgment when veering from the script

- Develop new approaches and strategies for delivering compelling presentations

- Effectively distinguish between features and benefits by selling the sizzle rather than the steak

- Maintain your mental focus when faced with rejection

- Effectively educate potential customers about the benefits and value of the company's services

- Demonstrate a greater ability to handle rejection, and maintain your enthusiasm when overcoming objections

- Close each call by asking for the sale

- Regularly follow up with customers to ensure high postsale satisfaction

- Focus on facilitating positive long-term customer relationships and high potential for repeat business

- Maintain all sales, quality, and performance standards as outlined in your scorecard

- Navigate effectively through our internal website to provide customers with accurate pricing, promotions, and service information

- Manage the customer sales cycle from initial interest through purchase
- Regularly scrub and update the sales force database recognizing the garbage-in/garbage-out rule
- Identify five new prospects per day through market and press research
- Execute follow-up mailings daily from 4:00 to 5:00 P.M.
- Customize boilerplate letters and mailings to targeted clients to work more efficiently and to save time
- Strengthen your scorecard results in the area of closing and getting commitment over the phone
- Act as a liaison between the customer and our credit and production departments
- Always communicate effectively, tactfully, and courteously with all clients and employees

High-Impact Verbs to Inspire Your Writing

urn to the following action verbs when looking for just the right word to craft goals for your employees. Verbs launch the action, and the right verbs will help you structure your ideas neatly and succinctly.

A
Accept
Acclimate
Accomplish
Account (for)
Achieve
Act (upon)
Adapt
Address
Adjust
Administer
Adopt
Advance
Advertise
Advise
Advocate
Aid
Align
Allocate

Allow
Amplify
Analyze
Anticipate
Apply
Appoint
Appraise
Appreciate
Approach
Approve
Arrange
Articulate
Assemble
Assess
Assign
Assume (responsibility for)
Assure
Attain
Attend

Audit
Augment
Authorize
Automate
Avoid

B

Balance
Broaden
Budget
Build

C

Calculate
Capitalize (on)
Capture
Catalogue
Categorize
Chair
Challenge
Chart
Clarify
Classify
Coach
Code
Collaborate (with)
Collect
Combine
Commit
Communicate
Compare
Compensate (for)
Compile
Complete
Comply (with)
Compose
Comprehend
Compromise
Compute

Conceptualize
Condense
Conduct
Confer
Connect (with)
Conserve
Consolidate
Consult
Contribute
Control
Convert
Convey
Convince
Cooperate
Coordinate
Correct
Correspond (with)
Counsel
Create
Critique
Cultivate
Customize

D

Debate
Debug
Dedicate (yourself to)
Define
Delay
Delegate
Deliver
Demonstrate (mastery of)
Design
Designate
Detect
Determine
Develop
Deviate (from)
Devise

Devote
Diagnose
Differentiate (between)
Direct
Disburse
Discipline
Discount
Discourage
Dispatch
Display
Disseminate
Distinguish
Distribute
Document
Drive

E

Edit
Educate
Elicit
Eliminate
Embrace
Emphasize
Employ
Empower
Enable
Encourage
Enforce
Engage
Engender
Engineer
Enhance
Enlist
Ensure
Entertain
Epitomize
Escalate
Establish
Estimate

Evaluate
Examine
Exceed
Execute
Excel (at)
Exercise
Exhibit
Expedite
Experiment
Exploit
Express

F

Facilitate
Familiarize (yourself with)
Focus (on)
Forecast
Formulate
Foster
Furnish
Further

G

Gather
Generate
Guide

H

Heighten
Highlight
Host

I

Identify
Illustrate
Implement
Improve
Incorporate
Increase

Individualize
Influence
Inform
Initiate
Insist (on)
Inspect
Inspire
Instill
Institute
Instruct
Integrate
Interact (with)
Interface (with)
Interpret
Intervene
Interview
Introduce
Invent
Investigate
Isolate (a problem)
Issue
Itemize

J
Justify

L
Lead
Lend
Leverage
Log

M
Maintain
Manage
Market
Master
Maximize
Measure

Mediate
Merge
Minimize
Model
Moderate
Modify
Monitor
Motivate

N
Navigate
Negotiate
Notify
Nurture

O
Observe
Obtain
Operate
Optimize
Orchestrate
Organize
Originate
Overcome
Overhaul
Oversee

P
Participate (in)
Perform
Persuade
Plan
Possess
Postpone
Prepare
Present
Prevent
Prioritize
Process

Produce
Program
Progress
Project
Promote
Propose
Protect
Provide
Publicize
Purge

Q

Qualify
Quantify

R

Recognize
Recommend
Reconcile
Record
Recruit
Rectify
Redeem
Redirect
Reduce
Refer
Refine
Refrain (from)
Register
Regulate
Reinforce
Reject
Rejuvenate
Render
Reorganize
Repair
Replace
Report
Represent

Require
Research
Resolve
Respect
Restore
Retain
Retrieve
Review
Revise
Revitalize
Reward
Risk
Route

S

Satisfy
Schedule
Secure
Seek
Select
Serve (as)
Share
Simplify
Solicit
Source
Specialize
Specify
Standardize
Stimulate
Streamline
Strengthen
Strive
Submit
Substantiate
Suggest
Summarize
Supervise
Supply
Support

Survey
Synchronize
Synthesize
Systematize

T
Tailor
Target
Terminate
Test
Thrive
Tolerate
Trace
Track
Transform
Translate

Trend
Troubleshoot

U
Unite
Update
Upgrade
Utilize

V
Validate
Verify
Volunteer

W
Welcome

Essential Adverbs to Get Your Message Across

Finding the right adverb to describe the action can sometimes be a challenge when drafting an employee's goals, so refer to this list often when structuring your thoughts and ideas.

A

Accurately
Actively
Adequately
Aggressively
Always
Appropriately
Assertively
Attentively

C

Calmly
Carefully
Cautiously
Clearly
Cleverly
Closely
Collaboratively
Commonly
Completely

Comprehensively
Conscientiously
Consciously
Consecutively
Consistently
Constantly
Constructively
Continually
Continuously
Correctly
Courageously
Creatively
Curiously

D

Deliberately
Deservedly
Diligently
Directly

E

Eagerly
Easily
Effectively
Efficiently
Energetically
Enthusiastically
Evidently
Exactly
Excessively
Extremely

F

Faithfully
Fervently
Frequently

G

Generally
Generously
Gently
Graciously
Gratefully

I

Immediately
Instantly
Instinctively
Intensely
Intentionally
Intently
Interestingly
Intermittently

K

Kindly
Knowingly

L

Lively
Logically
Loyally

M

Masterfully
Meaningfully
Mechanically
Methodically

N

Naturally
Neatly
Never
Normally

O

Objectively
Occasionally
Officially
Often
Openly
Optimistically
Overly

P

Partially
Patiently
Perfectly
Periodically
Playfully
Politely
Positively
Potentially
Powerfully
Precisely
Predominantly

Proactively
Productively
Proficiently
Progressively
Promptly
Properly
Punctually
Purposefully
Purposely

R

Rapidly
Readily
Reassuringly
Regularly
Reliably
Repeatedly
Respectfully
Responsibly
Routinely

S

Safely
Satisfactorily
Seemingly
Sequentially
Seriously
Sharply
Silently
Skillfully
Smoothly
Solidly
Sometimes
Specifically
Speedily
Spontaneously
Sporadically
Steadfastly
Steadily

Strategically
Strictly
Subjectively
Substantially
Successfully
Succinctly
Suddenly
Surprisingly
Swiftly
Sympathetically
Systematically

T

Tactfully
Tactically
Thankfully
Thoroughly
Thoughtfully
Timely
Typically

U

Ultimately
Unexpectedly
Uniformly
Unintentionally
Unnecessarily
Urgently
Usefully
Usually

V

Verbally
Vigorously
Voluntarily

W

Willfully
Willingly

Individual Development Plan (IDP) Tool

Instructions for Completing This Career Development Checklist

Development plans, by definition, should always be a two-way street, and your feedback is critical to your supervisor. This worksheet should be used to record what you would like to accomplish over the next 12 months. The purpose of this exercise is to help you focus on your immediate goals (with an eye toward your longer-term career aspirations), while providing your supervisor with important information in terms of how to best support you in achieving your self-identified goals. Please complete this self-evaluation form before your upcoming review, and be prepared to share your insights and recommendations with your supervisor in terms of timeframes and measurable outcomes. Use extra sheets of paper as necessary. Remember, as well, to refer to this IDP often throughout the upcoming 12-month review period to measure your progress.

A. Self-Assessment and Motivation (Where are you today?)

Choose two categories from the following six options in terms of what holds the most significance for you career-wise:

1. Career progression through the ranks and opportunities for promotion and advancement

2. Lateral assumption of increased job responsibilities and skill building (e.g., rotational assignments in other areas, overseas opportunities, and the like)

3. Acquisition of new technical skills (typically requiring outside training and certification)

4. Development of stronger leadership, managerial, or administrative skills

5. Work-life balance

6. Money and other forms of compensation

List two to three strengths and two to three areas for development, either based on your own assessment of your performance or on documented feedback from performance feedback sessions:

Self-Identified Strengths	Self-Admitted Shortcomings
1.	1.
2.	2.
3.	3.

B. Goal Identification (Where do you want to go?)

Identify two to three short-term goals that you want to achieve professionally over the next twelve months to help build your career and add value to our company. You may choose from any of the options in Section A above or create your own areas of interest. Include timeframes as well as the measurable outcomes to ensure that you'll have met those goals (if applicable).

Optional: Identify two to three longer-term goals (i.e., three to five years from now) that will help you progress in your career and satisfy your longer-term professional aspirations.

C. Goal Attainment (How will you get there?)

1. What specific actions do you see yourself taking to ensure that you achieve your self-identified goals?

2. What can your supervisor do to provide you with the appropriate amount of structure, guidance, and feedback to help you get there?

3. How can the company best support you and help you maximize your chances of success?

4. What points will you be able to add to your resume and/or self-evaluation in the upcoming review period as a result of this exercise to demonstrate concrete accomplishments, newly acquired skills, and/or an overall "achievement mentality" relative to the priorities you've identified above?

Optional: Would you like to share your resume with your supervisor as a career map and future guide to focus your career development efforts?

D. Next Steps and Follow-Up

Scheduled date to meet again to determine progress against your self-established goals and benchmarks: _____

E. Other

If applicable, please identify any areas of professional growth or self-development that haven't been addressed in this exercise, and that you'd like to address with your immediate supervisor.

Index of Particular Titles and Roles